# Picasso
# The Engraver

Cat. 39 **Marie-Thérèse in Profile/ Grand profil de Marie-Thérèse** Probably 1931
Monotype on copper covered with a tarlatan

BRIGITTE BAER

# Picasso
# The Engraver

*Selections from the Musée Picasso, Paris*

*with 126 illustrations*

Thames and Hudson
The Metropolitan Museum of Art

This book is published in conjunction with an exhibition at
The Metropolitan Museum of Art, New York
September 18 – December 21, 1997

The exhibition was organized in Paris by the
Musée Picasso and adapted for New York by
The Metropolitan Museum of Art

The exhibition is made possible by **GOYA** FOODS, INC.

Translated from the French by Iain Watson and Judith Schub
under the supervision of the author

Book design by Adam Hay, London

British Library Cataloguing-in-Publication Data
A Catalogue record for this book is available from
the British Library

ISBN 0-500-09269-9

Printed and bound in Hong Kong by C+C Offset

# Contents

# Foreword

Picasso, the foremost painter and sculptor of our century, is also its greatest printmaker. The more he is studied the more one perceives how intimately related are the life he lived and the images he created. Nowhere in his oeuvre is this better demonstrated than in his prints.

It is with pleasure that I introduce this selection of prints, which was presented in an exhibition by the Musée Picasso in 1996. In addition to intaglio prints, "Picasso Gravures: 1900-1942," the Paris exhibition, included the woodcuts and monotypes also shown in New York. In several instances, progressive states of individual images offer a rare opportunity to follow, step by step, Picasso's development of a specific theme.

On behalf of the trustees of The Metropolitan Museum of Art, I wish to thank Gérard Régnier, Director of the Musée Picasso, and the two organizers of the exhibition, Dominique Dupuis-Labbé, Curator at the Musée Picasso, and Brigitte Baer, compiler of the catalogue raisonné of Picasso's prints. Mme Baer's knowledge of Picasso's graphic oeuvre is prodigious, and she is the author of both essays featured in this publication.

Our extreme gratitude is extended to Goya Foods, Inc. for its important corporate underwriting of this exhibition. We would like to acknowledge, specifically, Joseph A. Unanue, its President.

**Philippe de Montebello**
*Director, The Metropolitan Museum of Art*

# Preface

Picasso passionately loved printmaking. We have only to consider his astonishing fecundity in that field. Between *El Zurdo*, the first plate he etched (1899), and the last one he did in Mougins on 25 March 1972, *La Femme au miroir* (*Woman with Mirror*), he produced more than 2,500 prints in various media – not including the states, of course. He was the most prolific printmaker of the twentieth century.

His inventiveness was prodigious. He worked on the prints with the same freedom he showed when confronted with every technique. Picasso was not a 'trained' etcher or engraver. But what did it matter? He attacked wood and metal without any *a prioris* and managed, through his 'finds', to enhance the opposition and marriage of black and white, as well as to obtain an extraordinary linear subtlety.

Above all, he shows us the wonderful world he created. Whether invented or rooted in his private life, a crowd of characters lives, loves, suffers and dies before our eyes. As Paul Eluard put it, it is a world where "he wants to win with gentleness through violence, and with violence through gentleness."

Perhaps it is not an exaggeration to compare the richness and complexity of Picasso's world, his reflections on life, love and death, with the one created by Balzac in *La Comédie humaine*.

More than his painting or drawing, printmaking gives us the feeling that for Picasso it was a kind of day-by-day private diary, telling us about his deepest emotions, his brooding on desire, suffering, separation, fear of old age and death. A kind of pillow-talk, an account, also an outlet and a therapy, his printmaking throbs so strongly with life that we can all of us, in our own ways, find while reading his 'picture-story' bits of our own lives. His magic wand allowed him to give a universal meaning to his most private feelings.

Of the overwhelming number of works that are available, we have had to 'extract' for exhibition a choice which best represents the Picasso iconography and his technical virtuosity. Hence the abbreviated period on which we focus: 1900-42. Brigitte Baer, author of the catalogue raisonné, *Picasso peintre-graveur*, a *magnum opus* which, with the publication of the seventh volume and the Addendum, is now completed, was kind enough to agree to organize this exhibition. The reader is sure to appreciate her unusual view of Picasso's themes and symbols, to which she gives us some of the keys, as well as informative notes on the artist's technique. We thank her for sharing with us the fruits of her intimate acquaintance with Picasso's work and for that passionate generosity which is her own.

**Dominique Dupuis-Labbé**
*Musée Picasso*

# Introduction

The aim of this exhibition is to entertain, not to teach. If it does teach, all the better. Those who wish to study Picasso's work in greater detail can do so by reading through the volumes of my catalogue raisonné, *Picasso peintre-graveur*. Given the large quantity of Picasso's prints in the Musée Picasso, a drastic choice had to be made, and I have made a very personal one, basically including only the prints I loved best, as well as some 'curiosities' for fun.

Prints have to be looked at closely. They are not things which can be absorbed rapidly. They demand a certain concentration. Hence it is impossible to take in more than a certain quantity at the same time. That is one of the reasons for choosing the period between 1900 and 1942. I, who know them all, would have dropped dead faced by the entirety of Picasso's print work, and even that of this limited period. Major surgery was necessary.

A large proportion of the exhibition is comprised of series of states, which is the best way to show how the artist worked, and how sometimes he changed his mind radically, thus changing the entire meaning of the 'image'. Picasso himself, once at least, said exactly the same thing. By limiting the number of prints, I hope that non-specialists, who are not obliged to look at every detail, can also share my pleasure in the beauty of these 'images'.

In my opinion, Picasso is the most important printmaker of the twentieth century. And even if there are people who think that, as is often the case with dead artists, for a certain number of years his paintings will be neglected or re-evaluated negatively, at the same time it is probable that his sculpture and printmaking will escape a similar fate.

While it is true that, for us, none of his prints has the evocative power of a good impression of the so-called fourth state of Rembrandt's *Three Crosses*, nevertheless *The Woman with a Tambourine*, for example, is a real 'vision'. But the reality of modernism cannot be denied and, perhaps in five hundred years' time when our era will be shrouded in ignorance, how will our descendants react when confronted with some of these prints? With stupefaction? With unease? Or with a kind of religious confusion? It is almost impossible to have the objectivity necessary to judge one's own era. In fact it is impossible. We are tempted to say: "We shall see about it later!" But of course we shall never see anything. Only later generations will be capable of seeing something.

If the Musée Picasso's collection of prints from the first half of the artist's life is extremely rich, that is because Picasso was like a squirrel hoarding away all the states, trial proofs and unique examples of his prints. So in 1979, at the time of the *Dation*,[1] the choice of prints for the Museum was not easy. The Bibliothèque Nationale had sent to Dominique Bozo, who was acting for the State (and to us who were working on the Picasso Estate), a list of the prints which they lacked – they had very little from the pre-War period – and it was in that context (*i.e.*, in the spirit of a 'National Collection') that the choice was made then.

There are several reasons to stop in 1942, which here means in fact the end of the Second World War, as Picasso from that date onwards hardly made any prints until 1945: the last one we show is from 1942. The reasons are of course the Second World War, then his mother's death. Also the end of the war constitutes for him a personal watershed. The Liberation of Europe was a liberation for him too, as it was the moment when he more or less broke off his relationships with the women who up until then had played such important parts in his life. At that time also he was gradually to escape from Paris towards the warm sunny South of

France. Moreover, from 1945 on, at least for some time, he devoted himself to lithography. Last but not least, in the post-war period he was no longer just an important artist but a 'star' and eventually he would even become a *monstre sacré*.

The catalogue is divided into two short chapters. The first is an attempt to explain what Picasso is talking about in his prints. The second deals with technique and how that impatient, inventive man used it. Like him, we have used simple language, deliberately trying to avoid any specialists' jargon.

For more than twenty years now, beginning with the work on the Picasso Estate and later during the period of my toiling on the catalogue raisonné, I have been in almost constant physical contact with Picasso's prints and plates. This has inevitably created an almost symbiotic relationship very different from that of other scholars who have not had that privilege and often basically know his work only via exhibitions and photographs or reproductions. In one sense this catalogue tells that story too.

Let us add that about 95 per cent of the sheets shown here are 'proofs' and not published impressions, and that many of them were pulled by Picasso himself, often in a happy-go-lucky way, just to 'see' the results of his work. They are all the more touching for not being perfectly printed.

And so, bon voyage!

Brigitte Baer

All references in the text and the checklist are to the catalogue raisonné of Picasso's prints, *Picasso peintre-graveur* (Berne, Editions Kornfeld). Bernhard Geiser, revised by Brigitte Baer (G/B): volume I (1990) and II (1992). Brigitte Baer (Baer): volume III (1986), volume IV (1988), volume V (1989), volume VI (1994), volume VII and *Addendum* (1996).

In the checklist, acquisition numbers of the Musée Picasso are cited as M.P.

All dimensions refer to the plate mark and not to the plate. Height precedes width.

Unless otherwise stated, all works belong to the Musée Picasso in Paris.

1. *Dation* in French law is a system whereby the State, after an artist's death, accepts works of art in lieu of death duties.

# A stream of pre-consciousness

If one were to conduct a sidewalk poll on Picasso's iconography – the sort of thing the media love – the majority response of the survey would without doubt be: "Oh, it's always women!" It is the same old story, isn't it? Gaia, Hera, Artemis, Aphrodite, the Virgin Mary… A painter paints the obsessions which irritate or disturb him. He dresses them up according to the role which they then play as a thorn in his flesh.

What puzzles people when they think about Picasso, the painter of women, is that he lived out half of his life during the so-called 'crisis of abstract art'. They tend to forget that until the age of twenty his roots were deep in the nineteenth century.

He would always say (since we are talking here about prints): "But it is only a print, nothing but a print, and a print without any title." And how right he was! Marcel Proust wrote that his *Recherche du temps perdu*, far from being the novel of society life which people imagined it to be, was merely the story of 'a vocation'. In the same way Picasso, at least in his printmaking, talks only of craftsmanship and work, 'art' if you like, even though art was a word he hated. Around 1927–30, as soon as he gave printmaking the role it was to keep until the end of his life, but especially up until the Second World War, his prints, like Caesar's *Commentaries*, are daily reflections, in his case full of subterranean cogitations, streams of consciousness, and of 'dream-things', which surface in a hidden way via images one can accept simply as beautiful pictures or else as subjects for thought or, better, for day-dreams. In fact, more often than not, they are loaded with meaning and are much more 'talkative' than the paintings and the sculptures he was making in the '30s. But they are talkative in the sense that Proust's narrator's strawberry tarts are talkative, speaking to him of his childhood (*Within a Budding Grove*).

In order to paint or sculpt a woman, one must decide, if one wants to paint what Picasso called painting (*i.e.*, art), on the way one looks at her and the 'angle of attack' which is chosen. I should like to introduce here an image of St Luke painting the Virgin, in which the disconcerting perspective brings home to us all the anxieties and doubts which a painter can have in relationship to his model. It is a painting in Prague by Jan Gossaert, called Mabuse, done around 1515, a rather late date for such a subject – which might explain the problems the painter had. At that time, perspective was a major preoccupation for artists, but Mabuse seems to use it in a hidden way in order to define for himself (and for us) all his unease and difficulties. For if you take up a

Jan Grossaert, called Mabuse, *St Luke Drawing the Virgin*, ca. 1515
(National Gallery, Prague)

normal position in front of that huge composition, you realize that the vaults, pillars and pavement are dancing and are not at all static. You yourself have to dance back and forth, up and down, from left to right, until finally you discover a limited point of view from which it all makes sense and stops moving. St Luke can only see his model from behind in three-quarters profile and he looks at the Virgin Mary and Child in a tiny mirror, which is an anachronism for the saint. Obviously, the mirror was the instrument of *artificialis perspectiva* but here, given the craziness of the results, it seems also to be the mirror-shield of Perseus in which Mabuse had no real confidence and which might be the mirror of our eyes if ever we have the patience to find those few square

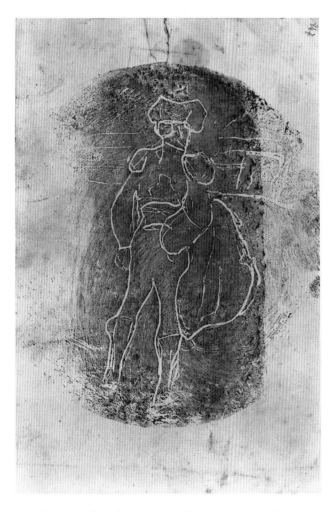

Cat.1 **Torero Seen from the Back/ Torero de dos** ca. 1900 Woodcut

inches from where the composition is at last in equilibrium. Now, for Picasso, the painter of 'emotion', perspective is a matter of outside/inside, external/internal objects where the created object itself is in between. And if he thinks about it while holding his pencil or his etching tool, he finds it a difficult thing to handle, as he always emphasized what he called 'respect for the object'.

But what object? Clearly this was not a new problem for him, but probably due to the work involved in 'his' *Chef-d'oeuvre inconnu* (1927–28) this difficulty would be partially resolved years later. All in all, the work on 'the artist and his model', which he treats rather simply in his illustrations for Balzac's text (and at the time he may not even have read it), must have been what Walter Benjamin called "an eddy in the river", an eddy which brings a lot of old mud and gravel up to the surface where they collide (*cf.* Proust's 'madeleine' or uneven paving stones). The amalgam that results is not a primal one but simply a screen-memory. Nevertheless, screen-memories stir the pre-conscious, generally evoking events or emotions which have been deeply buried because they were too painful and too hard to accept when they actually occurred.

It is only at the beginning of 1933 that Picasso in his print work begins to examine this problem (that of his relationship to the model), the sort of problem which often needs months or years to take shape in the conscious. More of a 'writing' for him than painting or sculpture, printmaking would be used to analyze or rather, given his character, to plunge into all this. He was to question his relationship to sculpture (his principal interest at the time), his relationship to the model, to the woman who is a kind of doppelgänger of the model, and also the relationship of both the woman and the model to his work and to him. Lastly, there was his questioning of the relationship of his sculpture to Renaissance and Baroque works and, perhaps more precisely, to Greek and Roman sculpture. At this moment, because he was no longer a young man and had achieved public recognition, because he had lived through the maelstrom of a passion, he had acquired

Cat. 2 **The Frugal Repast / Le Repas frugal** 1904 Etching and scraper on zinc, states I and II

sufficient distance not to be paralyzed any longer by the model's gaze. It is possible that he vaguely realized that a model is only a mould, or a fragment of a blank empty mould into which he was pouring his own emotions and fantasies. "They are, these women," writes Proust, "a product of our temperament, an image, an inverted projection, a negative of our sensibility… Our intuitive radiography pierces them, and the images which it brings back, far from being those of a particular face, present rather the joyless universality of a skeleton' (*Within a Budding Grove*, Scott-Moncrieff's classic translation). This skeleton *is* the model and also the lover who is not to be seen any more; it has to be clad with flesh and blood and brought to life if only perchance to sleep. Hence painting, sculpture and printmaking could create a "scrap of true life" (Proust) or endow this skeleton with "the quivering of life" (Picasso).

In fact, Picasso was all the more able to flesh out the skeleton and to fill the empty vase since, at least post-1910, he would never again draw, paint or etch from life. Somehow he would only look at the model inside himself via the sieve of his emotions. After two or three drawings 'extracted' from the model and thanks to his skill as a cartoonist, he would only retain those essential features which define its surface aspect despite any artistic shifts or emotional changes. Nevertheless, the person still had to remind him of herself by revolving around him as she shared brief moments in his day-to-day life, if only, as Proust put it, by stirring "the surface of the soul which otherwise would be in danger of becoming stagnant. Desire is therefore not without its value to the writer in detaching him first of all from his fellow men and from conforming to their standards, and afterwards in restoring some degree of movement to a spiritual machine which, after a certain age, tends to come to a standstill" (*The Captive*). In short, this is the 'emotion' Picasso is expressing.

After all, why should he use printmaking to give a shape to and analyze the questions and disappointments born of the model and her residual image, and of the woman who is its double? Perhaps it is only because of the mirror-image, of the inversion on the proof by the embedding of a copperplate into its damp paper. Does the plate turn into Perseus' shield?

In studying the series of prints dating from 1933–36, it is necessary to keep in mind one of Picasso's encounters (in Spanish *encontrar* means both 'to find' and 'to encounter'), the work he did to illustrate the *Metamorphoses* of Ovid. These totally flat line-prints which never deal with metamorphoses – Picasso's were more fantastic than those related by Ovid – portray plump classical bodies locked in love-making or in battles. Apparently both things meant the same to him. Yet what he discovered was that he could use his prints to tell stories, and he would make full use of this discovery when he busied himself first with his 'sculptor and model', and later when he put his minotaur on stage. Like the Ovid, this too was a commission and so a 'found object' which allowed him to speak about all the contradictions in human behaviour: body/soul, devil/angel, human/animal, adult/enraged child.

This method of using prints as a commentary and an interrogation did not occur to Picasso straight away. Between 1904 and 1932–33, his printmaking could be described as a kind of brook flowing along parallel to the river of his painting. He was not yet able to confide in the copperplate.

In 1904–05, his prints – in a purely linear way, as Apollinaire emphasized – deal with the same post-Symbolist topics as the rest of his work: acrobats, mountebanks, gypsies, but seen in their private lives as Manet had already depicted them in the *Gitanos*. Then comes the theme of life's sorrows in the well-known etching somebody dubbed *Le Repas frugal* (*The Frugal Repast*; cat. 2). Here symbols are piled on top of one another: bread and wine on the crumpled (altar?) cloth, blindness (a typical painter's malady, at least in Symbolist poetry), the couple forced together out of pain and sorrow but later driven apart, as underlined by the fact that "les deux tipes [sic]" (the two 'fellows'), as Picasso called them, turn their faces away from each other. Finally, the theme of Salomé (cat. 4), which, as is well known, is an offshoot of the Medusa theme. This motif, which would reappear under different guises until 1971 (see Baer 2010), is here still in its infancy. Picasso treats it in an ironical way, at least if we compare it to the Salomé of Gustave Moreau. No longer is Herod raised up on his throne in a dominating position, with Herodias tamely sitting at his feet; Picasso's Herodias is in control, erect, while poor fat Herod looks as if he were leaning on a kitchen table. Instead of being the focal point of the group, the head of John the Baptist has only his platter for a halo. And Salomé, stripped of her glittering jewels, dances a kind of cancan, tossing her leg up to the level of her raised arm (the raised arm in Gustave Moreau's *Apparition*). She looks like a May Milton by Toulouse-Lautrec (whose poster is pinned to the wall of the 1901 *Chambre bleue* [*Blue Room*]), but here is stark naked. Could she be 'catching her foot' (*en train de prendre son pied*, which is a common vulgar French expression meaning 'getting her kicks', to have an orgasm). The composition, cut on the bias like a wide ribbon across some dignitary's paunch, is all the more striking and beautiful because the sheet is very empty, so empty that the Delâtre workshop thought it was a good thing to halt the tone of the plate a centimeter short of the platemark. Picasso must have been hopping mad! It seems clear that the young painter – *o delectatio morosa* – superficially identified with the saltimbanques, the gypsies, with the lonely blind man and, of course, with John the Forerunner.

In 1906, however, it appears that he began 'to live things'. At Gosol, in the Catalan hill-country, after an always problematic visit to 'the parents' and also to his old pals, his painting seems to indicate that he fell in love with his charming girlfriend, Fernande, whom he depicts in a large tender gouache (Zervos I-310)[1]. Embarrassed at being painted in the nude, she blushes pink all over and her lips wear the semi-shy smile of a young virgin. At Gosol life was simple, full of non-intellectual pleasures, and there was old Fontdevila, a peasant pseudo-father figure. A 'scrap of true life' overflowing with happiness. There he forgot that

Cat. 3 **The Saltimbanques / Les Saltimbanques** 1905 Drypoint on copper, state II

existence is grey until it brutally shifted from pink to black partially because of another 'eddy in the river' – the fact that the old man's granddaughter caught typhoid fever, inevitably bringing up to the surface family alluvia and in particular the death of his own little sister. In short, there was the long journey back to the stifling heat of the Paris studio with everybody in a filthy mood and with no friends around (August in Paris!). Out of all this would come the two woodcuts which would 'Tahitize' and 'Gauguinize' Fernande, giving her a fixed, secretive, weird look: the *Half-Length Young Woman, Three-Quarters View* (cat. 8), the largest woodcut Picasso ever made and the *Half-Length Woman with Raised Hand* (cat. 7), which is a thinly disguised citation from Gauguin's work *Oviri*, "that strange, cruel, enigmatic monster… who spawned Seraphitus/Seraphita" – as Gauguin described it in an allusion to a story by Balzac.[2]

Cat. 4 **Salome / Salomé** 1905  Drypoint on copper, state III

Gustave Moreau, *The Appearance of John the Baptist's Head to Salome*, 1874–76 (Musée Gustave Moreau, Paris)

Cat. 6 **Standing Nude/ Nu debout, mains croisées derrière le do**s 1906
Monotype on glass

Cat. 5 **Fernande Olivier / Portrait de Fernande Olivier** 1906
Drypoint on copper

Paul Gauguin, *Oviri*, 1894 (Musée nationale des Arts africains et océaniens, Paris)

Cat. 7 **Half-length Woman with Raised Hand/ Buste de femme à la main levée** 1906 Woodcut

What a huge undertaking for Picasso, and a parano-melancholic one at that! He must have seen the stoneware *Oviri* in the Gauguin retrospective at the 1906 Salon d'Automne. Also, his friend Paco Durrio (in whose kiln he baked his sculptures at the time) owned an impression of the *Oviri* woodcut which Picasso could have looked at while waiting for his clay to be ready.

The face in his woodcut is truly enigmatic and the two crooked fingers recall precisely the hooked thumb on Oviri's thigh. They also look a little like a bird of prey's talons. Medusa is not far off.

The artist did not have much time in 1907 to devote to printmaking, apart from two small woodcuts, the two small birds he did to illustrate Apollinaire's *Bestiaire*. First of all, his rather cramped studio was invaded by women – Fernande who was not precisely the type of person who "passes through glances without breaking their absence".[3] Then there was the nine- or ten-year-old girl Fernande had temporarily 'adopted' as well as

Cat. 8 **Half-length Young Woman, three-quarters view/ Buste de jeune femme de trois quarts** 1906

Woodcut (Proof pulled by the artist in 1933)

Cat. 9 **The Eagle/ L'Aigle** (for Apollinaire's *Bestiaire*) 1907
Woodcut

Cat. 10 **The Chick/ Le Poussin** (for Apollinaire's *Bestiaire*) 1907
Woodcut

Fricka, the bitch, who chose this moment to produce a huge litter of puppies. Further, Picasso's brain and psyche were totally absorbed and invaded by the gestation of 'the big painting' which would eventually turn into the *Demoiselles d'Avignon*. A few words have to be said about this composition, famous for having pioneered what is called 'modern painting'. For after a long convalescence it transformed both the man and his approach to 'painting', which for him was synonymous with the whole of art, printmaking included.

When all is said and done, what is this painting but a gigantic Gorgon's head brandished in the face of the public? The shock still operates ninety years later: the visitors to the museum where it hangs in New York move quickly past it without really looking at it. Art historians, too, over-dissect the painting, clinging to details as if they were life-belts, as if they refused to let themselves be looked at by it. One can only admire the young man's courage during his solitary, self-inflicted ordeal. He fought to the bitter end and managed to dominate the elaborate images which, though buried, still lingered on during this crisis which some do not hesitate to label paranoiac. Since he was not mad, nobody found him "hanging by the neck behind his big painting" (as

Cat. 11 **Study for Nude with Drapery/ Etude pour** *Nu à la draperie* 1907

Woodcut

Derain is supposed to have said), but what a monumental artistic and psychic effort. Hats off to him!

Ushered on stage by an effigy of Fernande, here a kind of ringmaster, those four Demoiselles, who in fact are only one and who, of course, also reflect some facets of Fernande as Picasso saw her at that time, are Medusa, the Gorgon, a modern Gorgon whose presence is more terrifying than the ones painted by Caravaggio and Rubens. Has Picasso not made for himself, as well as for the rest of humanity, a dialectic image articulated in space from left to right and also situated temporally à la Proust? For in reality, although we see these ladies from the bottom up as if we were still small children on all fours (hence their elongation), they look straight into our grown-up eyes. And what a look! It combines a duple time: first, the mother's stare which, as far as the child is concerned, sees its unconscious desires despite the equally unconscious game-playing on the child's part, that piercing accusatory stare. Second, there is the absent, blind gaze (see the black blind eye of each woman), the gaze of the irate mother who sulks at her child – *i.e.*, refuses to *see* it. As is well known, only

Cat. 12 **Study for Standing Nude/ Etude pour *Nu debout*** 1907–08
Woodcut

*Les Demoiselles d'Avignon*, 1907 (The Museum of Modern Art, New York; Lillie P. Bliss Bequest)

22

Cat. 13 **Still Life with a Fruit Bowl/ Nature morte au compotier** 1908–09 Drypoint and scraper on copper, states I and III

through the mirror of its mother's eyes or face does the infant feel that it is alive. When the mother refuses to see her child, when she almost 'looks through' it, the child is no longer there and cannot 'integrate'. It ceases to live, undergoing a psychic death, at least temporarily. Thus, in some ways, she commits murder.

But to what sin does the child and do we owe that look? The half-supine woman gets up, towers over us, livid with anger and beautiful in her anger, for the sin is the sin of curiosity and the sexual desire hidden behind it, here symbolized by the fruit. Moreover, no doubt there must have been the curiosity of that convent-educated ten-year-old little girl in that confined space where no privacy was possible, and also Fernande's reactions to that curiosity which were so strong that in the end she would (she too!) abandon the child. Perhaps all this helped to clarify, to make real, in the artist's mind what had until then been rather ill defined. He made it clear in one of the sketchbooks pre-dating the definitive version of the painting. On one sheet, where

the second curtain behind which all the 'action' is taking place has the shape of a vulva, Picasso depicts a little toddler who is trying to worm his way in. The boy would vanish; his presence was too anecdotal. Not but what his unfortunate curiosity hampers the hidden couple's love-making. Then a most terrifying embodiment of a woman bursts on stage like a devil springing out of its concealed lair. The lower half of her face is misshapen, as if in the process of absorbing the penis of the hidden man (a frequent 'belief' and fantasy of young children). The woman on the right is the clumsy solution to the riddle of the 'fight' taking place behind the curtain, which the child only hears (this explains the choice of the 'big ear' for the squatting figure). She, the last Demoiselle, is a reference to the lute-player of Ingres's *Bain turc* who has 'an instrument between her legs'; she is also composed of bits of the face or mask of old Fontdevila. Further, she is shown in the position adopted by peasant women when they give birth in the fields (as in Gosol) or attend to the more

23

Cat. 14 **Still Life with a Bottle of Marc/ Nature morte à la bouteille de marc** 1911 Drypoint on copper

Cat. 15 **Seated Guitar Player/ Guitariste au fauteuil** 1911 and 1912

Etching and drypoint on copper, state IV/V

Cat. 16 **Guitar on a Table/ La Guitare sur la table** 1913–14

Woodcut, states I and II

common calls of nature. What was once ingested has later to be evacuated (another deep-rooted child's fantasy or 'belief' capable of assuming several shapes). She is a 'woman-with-a penis' as fantasized by the young child, an indelible image (the Demoiselles look straight into our grown-up eyes) and one which might account for the writhing snakes on the head of the Medusa. A lame solution, perhaps, but less frightening, even if it does not imply that one's private life is necessarily either satisfying or happy.

Anyway, it was a real crisis and a new awakening to awareness as well as an exorcism – not expressed in words but in images, then in a 'real painting' – of an iceberg-terror, nine-tenths hidden beneath the waters of the unconscious. In time, this confrontation so gallantly

and thoroughly worked out, would allow the young Picasso to lead an easier life and would permit the artist to continue to create in spite of a few fleeting mental blocks which he would escape from by cheating on himself.

So it was a great victory; but time would have to pass before this would be publicly recognized and he would be able to become whole again, to digest the change and to live, rather than just to survive.

After a more 'Jungian', hence less anxious-making, phase which produced the fine paintings in St Petersburg, Picasso, stimulated by his discussions and rivalry with Braque, was to plunge into a sort of affective, or emotional latency period out of which came Cubism. In this kind of highly 'intellectual' experience,

Cat.17 **Man with a Pipe/ L'Homme à la pipe** 1914 or early 1915

Scraper, etching and drypoint on aquatinted zinc, states II, III and VIII (enlarged)

Cat.18 **Two Women and a Nude Model/ Deux femmes regardant un modèle nu** 1923

Drypoint, scraper and etching on zinc, state III/V

the mind is so dominating that, just as a child learning to read and write leaves to one side the vital problems which previously obsessed him, the painter struggling to find a new way of seeing simultaneously lives through a moment of psychic and emotional calm which he was in need of.

From now on, even if he was not entirely rid of the Gorgon (but who is?), Picasso could and did control its impact by disguising it in a more acceptable way; and, like Perseus, he could use the severed head to paralyze others while remaining practically unscathed himself. So, whether it would take more or fewer lapses of time

after each confrontation, he was now capable of understanding and assimilating things. Perhaps finally he would acknowledge that a son of Medusa is quite like her and retains some of her power. Wasn't that something Parmigianino had grasped? And Caravaggio too! Picasso made use of this knowledge to play out the necessary pictorial variations in order to allow the public to accept and admire his work, even though they might still have had some misgivings.

Because they have been widely exhibited these last few years, a rather small number of Cubist prints have been included in this exhibition. However, I would like

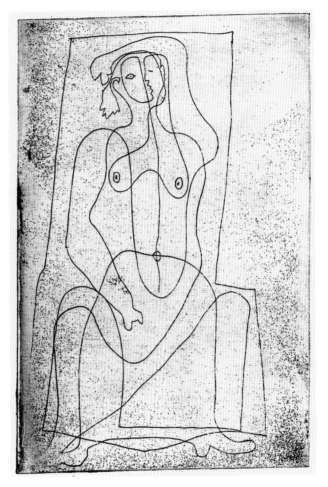

Cat.19 **The Race/ La Course** 1924–25

Etching on zinc

Cat. 20 **Seated Nude/ Femme assise, de face** 1924–25

Etching on zinc

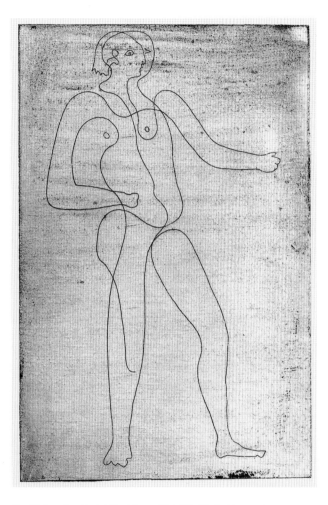

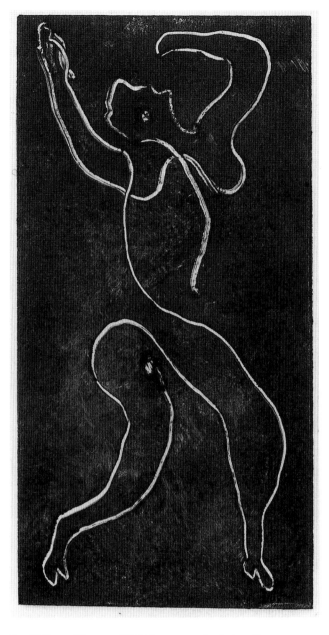

Cat. 23 **Standing Nude/ Nu debout. III** 1924–25 Etching on zinc

Cat. 26 **Dancer/ Danseuse** 1925 Monotype on zinc (enlarged)

Cat. 29 **Head of a Woman with Short Hair/ Tête de femme aux cheveux courts** 1925 Etching on zinc

Cat. 32 **Head of a Woman/ Tête de femme** 1925 Etching on zinc

to draw attention to the large and famous *Still Life with a Bottle of Marc* (cat. 14), which can be dated to autumn 1911. Paradoxically, one might say that Picasso 'regresses' here to Romanticism. In France, everybody knows (or knew) Fortunio's little song: "If you imagine that I will tell you/Whom I dare to love/Not for an empire/Would I name her."[4] Picasso, who was a painter and not a poet, in fact avoids painting his new love, the young woman he called Eva but who was in fact called Marcelle, yet he would 'name' her in this print, which dates from the period when they had just met. Clearly 'marc' is the beginning of her name and he adds the word 'vie' (life) for obvious reasons. Then there are the three playing cards: hearts the symbolism of which needs no commentary, clubs which are 'money' (he was no longer poor), and diamonds which, unless I am mistaken, mean 'new event' or 'surprise'. The composition, which was commissioned as a pendant to Braque's *Fox* is much more structured, tense, balanced, and stronger than Braque's work.

In the extraordinary small series of states of *Man with a Pipe* (cat. 17) from the end of 1914 or more probably early 1915, the image is freed little by little from the aquatinted background. At first it is rather ghostly, then it becomes more precise, with the use of the scraper, drypoint, etching needle. During this period Picasso drew and etched a series of men with hats, often seated at a table, reading a newspaper and smoking a pipe. Tobacco smoking is known to be a way of alleviating sadness, hunger, anxiety, 'nerves', etc. What is that man waiting for? For his friends to come back from the trenches? Or is it that implacable event of *jolie Eva*'s death because of her serious lung complaint?

After the war, during the time of the 'call to order', his printmaking sank into a profound morosity underlined by a veritable cohort of prints depicting three women, three bathers, the Three Graces or three goddesses (as in the judgment of Paris), who are rather plain and totally self-absorbed. I think that one can see here the beginning of a theme which Picasso was to use throughout his life: that of 'women together'. This is of course linked to the *Bain turc*, but also to his childhood,

Cat. 33 **Head of a Woman/ Tête sur un champ clair** 1925–26
Etching on zinc

when he was the only male in the totally feminine universe of his mother, aunts, sisters, female cousins and maids, who, as Kipling amusingly puts it "talked chiffons, which is French for mysteries". That must have been how the small boy in Malaga reacted, but there is an additional erotic connotation since Picasso was to return to the theme time and time again. We are showing only one example in order to illustrate the sort of monotype-like work done by the artist when inking the plate. It is *Two Women and a Nude Model* (cat. 18). Though difficult to make out in this beautiful unusual proof, the subject is not without interest: two ugly, badly dressed (but dressed) women have stripped the veils off a third very beautiful one, who is seen from behind, and leer at her with spite, contempt, reproach. Could it be Venus or, more likely, the wretched nymph Callisto? Who can tell?

Around 1924–25, Picasso, who had somehow acquired a sort of 'sketchbook' comprising about thirty-five identical (12 x 8 cm.) zincplates, began a series of etchings (and several monotypes) which are more interesting from the point of view of style rather than for their content. It seems fair to speculate that he had seen the series of small wonderful etchings done by Matisse, roughly between 1914 and 1916, in which the painter uses a few suggestive (à la Mallarmé), interrupted, and non-deliminating strokes to position asymmetrically a head of an often ugly woman so that it is cut by the edge of the plate. What might tend to confirm our hypothesis is the drawing of a head on page 5 recto of the Musée Picasso sketchbook no. 26, dated 1923 in the catalogue, which seems to have been 'lifted out' of the series by Matisse. Competition with (and in this case admiration for) other artists, and especially Matisse, was one of Picasso's favourite minor vices. Yet, when he actually stood in front of his 'zinc sketchbook', he did exactly the opposite and, more often than not, tried to draw the faces and bodies with a continuous line, not lifting his hand off the plate. He told Sabartés that he had got this idea from urchins on the beach at Malaga, who drew with a stick in continuous lines in the sand.

As I said earlier, without doubt it was all the effort involved in the illustrations for the *Chef-d'oeuvre inconnu* which triggered his use of printmaking to clarify his relationship both to his work and to the model. In short, the 'study sheets' in the book are much more successful than those which depict the artist and his model. Does that mean that a work of art is more beautiful than reality?

After a beautiful parody of Italian Futurism, *The Death of the Bull* of 1929 (cat. 34), in which any *aficionado* can really believe he is 'seeing' the final moments of that amorous combat between bull and man[5] – a trial run for the illustration of the first idea for the *Tauromaquia of Pepe Illo* – follows the long series of prints for the Ovid. For obvious reasons, we have chosen to show the first one Picasso worked on, *The Death of Orpheus*, together with its three preliminary stages: first a preparatory drawing, very rare in Picasso's work, followed by the extraordinary, tense, frightening, savage drypoint (cat. 36), whose rhythm was to be partially repeated in the important etching of 1934, *Great Corrida with Female Matador* (cat. 62). Then follows the heavily worked etching which is softer and suppler but where the Maenads are equally terrifying, as if born out of the head of someone with persecution mania (cat. 37). Finally, there is the last composition, very close to the other illustrations which were to be used in the book (cat. 38). In the first two versions, bullocks/bulls play a major part. As for the Maenads, they are already those which Picasso would use in 1939 (*The Woman with a Tambourine*) and in 1944 (coloured drawing after Poussin's *Bacchanal* in the Louvre): the embodiment of hand-to-hand fighting in the streets.

In November and December 1932 there began a series of very small prints with bathing women as a subject which allows us to catch a glimpse of the profile of Picasso's new model, Marie-Thérèse. For once the prints even seem to be linked to real events, since in fact the young woman was only interested in swimming. The repeated drowning theme appears to be a parody of Molière's "*Qu'allait-il donc faire dans cette galère?*" (What on earth was he doing in that galley?)[6]. Picasso had bumped into her on the street at the beginning of 1927 (at least so he said!) when she was just eighteen years old. He then installed her in the rue La Boétie, just down the road from his own apartment, when she became legally of age at the end of 1930. She never 'drowned', but she had caught an illness carried by rats when swimming in the Marne: high fever, hospitalization and the loss of most of her yellow hair. She was more or less convalescent during the first months of 1933 and so less often with him, which allowed him to take stock of the situation. Since she had lived previously in the suburbs, she had been rather like the 'Fugitive' of Proust's narrator but a 'fugitive' who swam rather than rode a bicycle and who wore a beret instead of a polo-cap. She was resplendent with that 'youthful devilish beauty' which Picasso loved, although he perhaps preferred the prettiness of the adolescent thirteen-year-old girl he had never known, with her fluffy hair waved on purpose to fit under a round hat for a photograph taken in 1922 which the artist carried in his wallet. But then, she had turned into Proust's 'Prisonnière' for, although she did not live with him, he could always drop in on her whenever he felt inclined. As she had been educated mostly abroad, she had no school-chums, no friends and no social life apart from her mother and one dark-haired sister, Geneviève, whom she loved. She cordially disliked her other sister, Jeanne, who incidentally was a blond. Hence, she led a very secluded and lonely life (like Caroline in Balzac's *Une double famille*). Now, somebody who has a prisoner feels somewhat imprisoned himself, even if he has elsewhere another family and a professional life with his pals, friends and various acquaintances. It appears that the young woman had no particular desire to share that life and Picasso realized full well that she would never fit into it, as she was not interested in art, nor in his work, nor in the fashionable intellectual movements of his artistic-cultural circles. Rather quickly, Marie-Thérèse had turned into a sturdy athletic woman but, up until the end, Picasso would continue to paint her as he had first seen her, just as Proust's narrator continues to love and try to discern in Albertine the young girl with the black polo-cap and plump cheeks who had fascinated him at the start. It is all very well to put a bird in a cage but it never remains the same bird, and that is perhaps what Picasso is trying to show us with the well-known *Girl before a Mirror* of 1932 (Zervos VII-379). Here again let me quote Proust: "But this calm which my mistress procured for me was an assuagement of suffering rather than a positive joy. Not that it did not enable me to taste many joys… but I tasted these joys on the contrary when Albertine was not with me" (*The Captive*). And it is worth repeating that Picasso never painted, drew, sculpted or etched from life but when the model was absent and that, as for Proust's narrator, love for him was mostly made up out of jealousy. But he loved her.

I apologize for these 'biographical' details but they seemed necessary at this point. To recapitulate, in his printmaking during the first months of 1933, Picasso was thinking about himself and his relationship to his model. During the second half of January, while his hand and conscious attention were focused on his work, he mulled over in his mind the manifold facets of the model, who was also his mistress. His anxieties and doubts are betrayed by the enormous amount of work he put into one small copperplate, *Flute Player and Sleeping Woman*. This began with a series of about thirty monotypes, followed by thirty-one states in drypoint and continued with another fifteen monotypes (cat. 45, 46). The model, who in the drypoint is closer to the young girl of 1922, or at least to the sinuous young woman of 1927 rather than to the woman Marie-Thérèse had become, is doubled: on the one hand, there is a sleeping woman – sleep which guarantees the tranquil calm possession of the 'object' with closed eyes; then there is also a woman playing the flute who, identical to the sleeping one, keeps a vigil and is therefore thinking. Of freedom? Of the sexual pleasures the flute might symbolize? Or is she only the opaque dream of the sleeper?

It is interesting to note that the first monotype depicts the female flute-player as a boy or perhaps a Marie-Thérèse without hair. There are no major changes in the drypoint, which gradually becomes more complex by the simple addition of a multitude of lines, but the monotypes which follow transform the two young girls into a variety of plant life or algae-like conglomerations, before the artist 'terminates' them in two rather heavy sculptures, redolent with sexual protuberances. It is as if the engraver wondered what the model was and what this model meant to him. A melancholy rather than happy train of thought.

Far more intellectually stimulating and exciting is the drypoint begun shortly afterwards on 18 February, a study of a flattened sculpture, squashed on to the plate and in turn ironed flat on the proof by the plate. This is *Sculpture. Head of Marie-Thérèse* (cat. 48), worked on in

Cat. 34 **The Death of the Bull/ La Mort du taureau** 1929 Etching on copper

twenty states and four monotypes (cat. 49). It is based on the four monumental plaster heads of Marie-Thérèse which Picasso had modelled at Boisgeloup some eighteen months earlier during the summer of 1931. The idea was probably triggered by Brassaï's photographs of the Boisgeloup sculpture studio (in fact, the stables) done in 1932. One of these photographs, taken in the uncanny light of Picasso's car headlights, is a phantom-like apparition showing three of these plasters (see Spies 131, 132, 133)[7], like the heads of the three Gorgons, one of which has the swollen, glaucous and empty eyes which Picasso re-uses from the ninth state onwards of his engraving.

State by state, beginning with a simple left profile followed by a three-quarters one, the head turns to the right, as if transformed by the addition or subtraction of lumps or rolls of plaster; it is as if the artist himself prowled around the head or spun it round on a turntable – all this in his mind, since he was actually in Paris – in order to criticize it and to amalgamate the four plasters into a single flat image of a new sculpture which would synthesize them all. By flipping through the sheets as if they were a flip book, we have the sensation that we too are spinning the sculpture round in order to look at it from almost every angle. But still the head never loses sight of us. We are cornered by its eyes as the artist himself was cornered. The primordial whiteness of the sculptures had already created an immense distance between them and the model. Here the artist steps back and criticizes his own work. There

Cat. 35 **Study for** *The Death of Orpheus* (Ovid's *Metamorphoses*)/
**Etude pour** *Mort d'Orphée* 1930 Pen and ink on paper

Cat. 36 **The Death of Orpheus, I** (Ovid's *Metamorphoses*)/
**Mort d'Orphée. I** 1930 Drypoint on copper

is also a lot of what Merleau-Ponty[9] speaks of as double spatio-temporal distancing : a distance defined by touch (skin, plaster) and the mourning over it. Then there is the transformation of a totally round object into a flat 'thing'. Further, there operates the reversed mirror-image of the 'drawing' on the copperplate when the damp paper is pressed on it. Then there is yet another distancing, that of the created object, the plasters, which once perhaps 'belonged' to the artist but now are 'free', thus redoubling the gap between them and their gestation.

What we have before our eyes in the final state is a kind of ghost-sculpture knitted out of most of the threads of the pentimenti, just as the wax under the celluloid of a magic slate is incised. But it is also a "dialectic image" (to use Walter Benjamin's term) which looks at us, as it had looked at the artist, an image which

has a presence, a profound ugly beauty, an 'aura' that in a strange way the well-known related drawing lacks, perhaps because it is too mannered and manneristic. But it is also a kind of Medusa's head, as well as an image full of mourning, for, as Proust said somewhere, we are dying practically every day. The sculptor who made those four heads is dead: he is no longer the same and will never execute this new sculpture. The man himself died each time his desire to touch the plaster, to touch the model, died and has been reborn as an other. The model too, the one of 1931, is dead, on the one hand because the sculptor's desire changed, on the other because *she* changed. Girls do change between the age of twenty and twenty-two; indeed, they changed more quickly at that time, and also the model was one of those women who mature rapidly. So, like the series of 'portraits' of sculptures done afterwards, our head is a

36

Cat. 37 **The Death of Orpheus, II**/ **Mort d'Orphée. II** 1930 Etching on copper

Cat. 38 **The Death of Orpheus, III/ Mort d'Orphée. III** 1930 Etching on copper

kind of funerary stele, as shown on a tiny print that Picasso worked and reworked at length (cat. 42C) – a minute etching which is visible at the left top center of a proof which groups four of the small prints from this period – but here the nearly identical head is planted on top of a marble column partially covered by tendrils of ivy. Ivy is the symbol of everlasting memory (*Je meurs où je m'attache*, i.e., I die where I cling). On one of the other copperplates with sculpted heads, the artist even included something like a relic since he 'drew' it with Marie-Thérèse's nail varnish.

Then we come to the rather simple iconography of the first half of the series called 'Suite Vollard'. These compositions arrive at a more superficial anecdotal complexity, now showing not only the relationship of the artist to his sculpture (which comprised all his other work) but also that of the artist to the model and to sculpture. It is also a question of the relationship of classical sculpture to his own sculpture, personified by one of these heads; further, there is the attitude of the model to the sculptor and to sculpture in general.

Until the introduction of his minotaur into the story in May 1933, Picasso continues to etch images, all of them tending to show more or less the same thing: the sculptor most of the time does not look at the model but only at his sculpture, and the sullen, drowsy, sulking model has generally the empty eyes of the women in the *Bain turc*. Or else, the sculptor examines a pseudo-classical group (there is never any exact reference to specific sculptures) as if wondering whether the metamorphoses of his own sculpture stand comparison with classical sculpture. Or the model stares in amazement at one of these heads, supposed to represent her, which does not assuage her narcissism as a 'real portrait' might do, and which in fact she neither understands nor is at ease with.

One of the etchings, *Muse montrant à Marie-Thérèse pensive son portrait sculpté* (*Muse Showing Marie-Thérèse Her Sculpture-Portrait*, G/B 299), really seems to be a product of one of the etcher's bad moods when confronted by the model's lack of understanding of his work, hence of his life. At least at the start, the model is a viciously true representation of a Marie-Thérèse not transformed by art. It shows a heavy, badly dressed woman, seen in an awkward position, her feet clumsily turned out, who is looking with sadness and even despair at one of the plaster heads which is supposed to 'deify' her. Picasso was to retain this image for three states, then, perhaps ashamed, made the model unrecognizable by schematizing it with drypoint.[8]

In two etchings, however, the sculptor is looking at his model. One dated 7 April 1933 shows a still androgynous teenage girl with faun's ears. The other, done the day after, is more seductive and complex. It is *Sculptor and Model with a Mirror* (cat. 52), in which the sculptor, a very good looking man, scrutinizes, with the fond, amused and mysterious smile Humphrey Bogart gives Lauren Bacall in their early movies, the model who had made a great effort to look pretty by having her hair curled. She is looking at herself in a mirror propped against a sculpted head of the sculptor. What does she see there? What is it which prompts the ambiguous glance of the sculptor? It is certain that she cannot perceive anything but one of these plaster heads she does not appreciate and which she does not want to know anything about.

In April 1933, Picasso had to create a minotaur for the cover of the first issue of the magazine with that name. He had no problems in fitting a bull's head on a human body, and certainly he did not draw any inspiration from photographs of Cretan sculpture which he had never seen. His unique problem was whether or not to provide the beast with a tail. But this minotaur was to serve him over and over again as a vehicle to express the contradictory elements of his nature: love, passion, tenderness and rage. When he introduces this highly personal character in his graphic story-telling, it follows several sheets which represent violent embraces, almost battles, between two figures nearly transformed into some kind of beasts. He could not go on for ever etching mating-scenes in contrast to 'the repose of the sculptor' and so on. The minotaur was to synthetize all this, since as a man he is gentle and as a bull full of rage. It simply depends on his mood. But the minotaur has a double, a thinking creative man, the sculptor and the painter; and from March 1934 onwards he is replaced by a young man half-hidden behind a minotaur's mask. A print begun in June 1933, *Marie-Thérèse Dreaming of Metamorphoses* (cat.55), the first state of which depicted, as was normal for the series, the model day-dreaming between a minotaur and a sculptor, was to be worked on again at the end of 1934 and then, as in a fairy tale, the minotaur turns into an effeminate, highly made-up young Greek actor, with his false tail attached to his belt and his minotaur mask in his hand. A second representation of Marie-Thérèse appears behind the sculptor, but her role is confined to that of a friend and a muse. This seems to mean that passion, personified by the minotaur, is gradually fading away. In addition, Picasso resumes the 'mating' theme, but the two figures are now more like machines than human beings. Their embrace becomes both animal and mechanical (cat. 57).

In 1934, too, the bull returns to the scene and the model becomes a female matador who swoons on its back – in short, a post-coital image. In June 1934, a very large etching (cat. 60) parodies and lampoons this theme, turning it into an elaborate joke. The bull has sentimental eyes and a human mouth and nose; it also seems to have its head wreathed with tinsel off a Christmas tree which is in fact merely the embroidery on the sleeve of the female matador. But isn't all that very 'sugary' for Picasso? Back from his summer holiday in Spain with wife and son, oddly enough the artist attacks another big etching of the same size, *Great Corrida with Female Matador* (cat. 62), and creates an image of total paranoia: the same female matador and the same bull, but this time in an arena and hysterical with pain and fury. A crowd of spectators, *peónes* and picadors mills about in an amorphous mass. Also, there is no air, no proper distance, hence no perspective. The rhythm of this superb achievement reminds us of the murderous madness of the Maenads on the first plate of *The Death of Orpheus*, but here it is against the poor bull that the mob vents its fury. What was the crisis which triggered this? It cannot just have been Olga's howlings and wailings, to which Picasso was quite accustomed.

We shall never know and it has no importance whatever, but that does not prevent us from admiring one of his finest prints.

When the minotaur reappears at the end of 1934, the poor thing has altered a great deal. He has grown old, is blind and helpless, and like Oedipus leaning on his staff, is being led into the unknown by a little girl who first has the fluffy hair of the adolescent Marie-Thérèse in the 1922 photograph, but later is given the schematic profile which the artist assigned to the young woman. It is an image of wretchedness and, even worse, of total dependency and decline. A young sailor, who is also Picasso, looks coldly on, as if one part of the man, the artist, still kept his feet on the ground. It is the young sailor who will win at the cost of much suffering: it is the beginning of the end of a great love-story. Three months later, at least in the artist's more or less unconscious mind, the sacrifice was accomplished.

Between 23 March and 3 May 1935, Picasso was to struggle with his most famous print, *The Minotauromachy* (cat. 68). Though this is a very puzzling image, I think we should opt for the simplest possible interpretation. The composition is rather like a curtain call: all the 'creatures' which have haunted the prints for two years are present and on stage, and the artist had no need to go fishing for inspiration or 'shapes' in Old Master painting and sculpture to add or subtract anything at all either from his actors or from the play which unfolds before our eyes. Marie-Thérèse, the female matador, not disarmed (an important detail), the lover, is on the point of exiting the stage since she is about to become a mother (see the wound in the side of the mare, on which she is lying and which is also her double). This change necessitates a different type of emotional attitude. The sculptor is halfway up a ladder, not dissimilar to the one Picasso had in the Bateau-Lavoir when painting his *Demoiselles*, but which might also be the ladder used in Christ's Descent from the Cross (hence the vehicle of the final act of the Passion/passion, in both parallel senses of the word). He is escaping over the wall to other pastures, other sources of inspiration (for a certain time Picasso would practically abandon sculpture). Yet he still looks over his shoulder as if to imprint on his memory the image of that body he had so loved to depict. Weighed down by a heavy bundle, the minotaur comes to make his last bow, longing for the bracing sea air. The little girl, with her curly hair, round hat and sober long-sleeved dress is a nearly exact replica of the 1922 photograph of Marie-Thérèse at thirteen. She carries the flowers Marie-Thérèse adored and perhaps also 'her flower', the flower of an eighteen-year-old virgin. By the light of her candle (there was hardly any electricity at Boisgeloup), she shows the female matador to the minotaur as if saying, "What have you done to me?", while he hides his face from the flame (shame? guilt?), but also refracts the light back on to the child, the true object of his love.

In the tower, perched in the arched window, are the model and her double – one might almost say the sleeping woman and the woman flute-player of 1933. The two of them are entirely concentrated on feeding pigeons, oblivious to what is taking place below at ground level. Might this tower not be an 'ivory tower', cut off from the world, a place where the artist had lived with his model/mistress, an ivory tower which eventually could not but make that bond a shade too oppressive and confined?

A thunderstorm is brewing in the sky and it is beginning to rain. The worst year of his life was what Picasso called this period. If he wanted to continue painting, he needed a breath of fresh air, and for him painting was life itself. Nevertheless, he would remain fond of the young woman and look after her and their child. He would do other portraits of her. But his life and inspiration were about to change; in fact the change had occurred during the gestation of *The Minotauromachy*.

One day, however, when Picasso came back to Paris in the spring of 1936 after a brief stay in Juan-les-Pins with the mother and infant girl, Marie-Thérèse would once more be his model, the model for the *Faun Unveiling a Sleeping Woman* (cat. 60). It was probably inspired by Rembrandt's etching of *Jupiter and Antiope* rather than by the Ingres version of the same subject.

Not only was the small painting by Ingres of mediocre quality and thus unlikely to have caught his attention, but from 1934 onwards, as Kahnweiler relates, Picasso was obsessed by Rembrandt's 'blacks' (*cf.* cat. 58).

The composition may be considered by some to be rather anecdotal and romantic, but it remains one of the artist's major prints. And – not that that adds to or subtracts anything from it – Picasso worked on it like a lunatic, using one after the other all the different techniques of aquatint. The last state gives us a truly romantic image with its lunar lighting, the faun's beauty and the subtle way light and shade are played with.

But let there be no mistake: the 'picture' is not, as might appear at first sight, a secular Annunciation, not an awakening but rather a re-awakening to reality and also an adieu. A faun is lustful, whereas the minotaur was capable of passion and occasionally of being in love. Moreover, Antiope's story puts in a nutshell that old women's adage: ten minutes pleasure followed by twenty years of pain. The face and all the upper part of the sleeper's torso remain in semi-darkness. The faun only sees (and in fact only unveils) the young woman's stomach and breasts, as well as a huge pair of lightly shaded buttocks. An allusion to the belly which carried the baby and to the breasts which suckled it? Or is it merely a reference to an exclusively physical desire focused entirely on the most erotic parts of the body, in fact to a faun's obsessional desire? Perhaps it may also be a farewell to and a regret for that desire itself? Or else a dream dreamt by the sleeper?

Shortly afterwards Picasso found another source of inspiration, another model who, no doubt, coincided more directly with his mood at that time: a stylish young woman with an apartment and a job of her own, who often saw friends of his like the Eluards, and who was part of that floating bohemian group he liked to meet with in cafés and bistros where they talked endlessly about art, poetry and current events. Dora Maar was a photographer. Certainly it was the life-style the artist needed then, at least for a time. Just as in the Braque-Eva period, he formed a kind of team composed of his life-long friend Sabartés who, by November 1935, had moved into the rue La Boétie, and a girl-friend who spoke Spanish. With each of them he could lead a social life and make a break not only with Olga and the divorce but also with the secluded life he had led with Marie-Thérèse.

In addition, Dora Maar – even those who met her only after 1945 still say so – was 'brilliant' and 'fascinating', and in the first engraved portrait he made of her, the artist especially emphasizes her sparkling eyes, framed in luxuriant eyelashes, and her delicate features. Moreover, Dora Maar was not a young naive girl, since any woman who had lived for a while with the writer Georges Bataille could not have escaped being 'awakened' and intellectually stimulated by him.

And then there was the political upheaval in Europe, and particularly the Civil War in Spain, where Picasso could no longer go but where his family still lived. The images he produced at the time in his prints are much more 'open' in the sense that they are composed out of a great variety of elements which, although very eclectic, are so well blended that one has the feeling of looking at simple, almost spontaneous compositions.

After a clever technical experiment – the etching he did on a halftone plate made from a photograph taken in his studio to illustrate the special 1935 issue of *Cahiers*

Cat. 40 **The Diver/ La Plongeuse** 1932 Etching on copper, printed with collage in 1936

*d'Art* devoted to him – the artist was to begin work on two of the large prints which are among his most beautiful and famous ones.

The first is the large *Weeping Woman* (cat. 71), two impressions of which (one of the third state and one of the seventh) were hung alongside *Guernica* in the Spanish Pavilion at the 1937 International Exhibition in Paris. Even if Picasso said to Malraux that it really depicted Dora Maar,[10] we must not forget that the artist broadened the subject (we are back to Proust's 'skeleton' which has to be clad with flesh and blood) by immediately adding that he felt that women were "machines born to suffer". Roland Penrose relates – long before all those 'Picasso-told-me' invented stories – that the artist had mentioned to him at the time a letter he had received from his mother, describing her life during the street-fighting of 1937 in Barcelona: she wrote that her face was continuously blackened by the smoke of the burning houses and churches and that her eyes were perpetually filled with tears. This connotation seems present at least in the two last states of the print. In the sixth, the artist blackens with vigorous tight drypoint strokes the eye-sockets, the nose, the upper lip, the cheek and the handkerchief of his weeping woman, then in the seventh state 'cleans' her up in order to obtain more definition and to give more prominence to the tears.

And then, as usual, there is also another 'family story' involved. Sabartés relates that Picasso's father had once 'broken' and reshaped a small, cheap plaster-of-Paris bust of an Italian peasant woman (the Picasso family is said to have been vaguely of Italian extraction). He had added to it a kind of veil and tears made out of glass beads, thus transforming it into a typical Spanish *Mater dolorosa*.

The fact is that the *Weeping Woman* is a composite image, but it was easier to answer Malraux that yes, he was right; it was Dora Maar (which indeed it was) – all the more so as Picasso was surely only half-conscious of the emotional impact of his print.

More than all his other prints, the second great etching translates a 'vision' despite or rather because of its simplicity. It is the bacchante, the maenad called *The Woman with a Tambourine* (cat. 78). It is more than probable that this dates from the second half of January 1939. The print is an exceptionally composite, variegated image in spite of the limpidity of the final result. In order to grasp this, we have to follow its evolution step by step. In the first state, Picasso borrows the lower part of the body, the lowered arm apparently leaning on the shadow of a chair, as well as the distribution of the light and dark areas created by the furiously etched strokes (grained and thus giving an impression of pastel) from a monotype by Degas worked over with pastel, *Après le bain* (Lemoisne 717).[11] Picasso must have seen it either in a book by Vollard (published by Crès in 1924) or at the major Degas exhibition of 1937 in the Orangerie, or more likely both.

We must take into account the inversion of the 'drawing' on the copperplate when seen on the proof and also the habit Picasso had of turning over, like a pancake, the figures he lifted out of other painters' paintings. Seen from behind in Degas's monotype, the woman is seen here from the front (*n.b.* the back, in any case, was part of Marie-Thérèse iconology). Thus the image created in the first state is, if one excludes the idea of the bacchante, a sort of disguised citation of Degas, particularly if we do not overlook the foot squashed to provide equilibrium so frequent in the paintings and drawings of Degas's dancers.

Without the support of the back of the chair there is no equilibrium and this woman cannot stand upright and keep her balance. Picasso, who found ways to stabilize his most acrobatic figures, could not but notice it. However, he would try against all odds, for two very subtly worked new states, to give stability both to his woman and to his composition, while retaining her awkward position. It is only in the fourth state that he turns to Poussin, probably to the Maenad in the London *Bacchanalia*, in order to throw back the leg of his bacchante, thus finally achieving balance for the woman and the whole composition. She now looks like a great exotic butterfly pinned to a black velvet background. But Picasso still went on with the obsessive

Cat. 44 **The Storm/** *L'Orage* 1933 Etching on copper

search for equilibrium so typical of Degas, violently scraping the leg in the air to disengage it from the background, simultaneously repositioning the buttocks. He is doing nothing else but paying a kind of tribute to the way Degas worked on his 'black monotypes', gradually wiping away with a rag to free his figures, etc., from a uniform black-inked plate.

But, as Picasso once said, even painters have fathers and mothers. Here the father is personified by the citations of 'the masters'. And the mother is equally present, even if he was barely conscious of his references to her. It so happened that on 13 January 1939, at dawn, while she was modestly dressing behind the half-opened door of a wardrobe (the beds being full of children), the old lady lost her balance, fell down and broke her spine. She died before nightfall. The fighting was then at its height in Barcelona, only ten days before Franco's troops entered the city in triumph. Precarious stability, research for equilibrium in an impossible position… Could it not be for these reasons that Picasso toiled on, obstinately trying to keep his 'woman at her toilette', and his dancer, in her initial pose? And then art takes over and the bacchante becomes what she is, taking on a new meaning and becoming an evocation (according to Picasso) of hand-to-hand combat in the streets. Poussin's Maenad fits in well here. The hand with the grapes becomes the lowered hand in the etching; the wind-swept hair corresponds to the wild locks of Picasso's bacchante. And yet, at the same time in the artist's mind the model is still somehow or other Dora Maar. "And when inspiration is born again, when we are able to resume our work, the woman who was posing for us to illustrate a sentiment no longer has the power to make us feel it. We must continue to paint the sentiment from another model, and if this means infidelity towards the individual, from a literary point of view, thanks to the similarity of our feelings for the two women, which makes a work at the same time a recollection of our past loves and a prophecy of our new ones, there is no great harm in these substitutions" (Proust, *Time Regained*, tr. Andreas Mayor).

If we try to go a little further, isn't the mother of the artist's childhood still present here? Anyone who has seen a happy young mother dancing out of pure joy in front of her fascinated first-born can understand that, in certain cases at least, the very idea later on of her dancing for or with someone else dismays the grown-up child: hence the hand-to-hand fighting, the maenads, Salomé and perhaps also the *Demoiselles*.

Picasso is quoted as saying half-jokingly to Malraux, "When I paint a woman in an armchair, the armchair is old age and death, eh?"[12] Dora Maar is par excellence the painter's and the etcher's Woman-in-an-Armchair. To be sure she had her bouts of melancholy like him, but all the same… there is something bizarre in the two prints of 1939.

The first Dora Maar in an armchair, of 1938, was regal and monumental in spite of the small size of the plate, and even more so after Picasso had agreed to suppress his scribbling underneath. He struggled through ten states with this print of a seated woman destined for

André Breton's *Anthologie de l'humour noir* (cat. 77), but the chair is barely visible. Then, in the early months of 1939, the artist twice depicts a woman in an armchair who looks totally miserable and weighed down by sorrow. For this exhibition, we have chosen the finer but more sinister one (cat. 89). If you like, it is Dora Maar, but only because she was his model at that time, with the angular lobster-like form he gave her whereas he painted Marie-Thérèse as a soft, sluggish, smothering octopus. The woman clings to the arms of the chair, and her feet, instead of touching the ground, are suspended in mid-air with the soles of her shoes astonishingly prominent, as if she had been dragged there and could not sit upright. Is that not old age and death? When Picasso's mother fell down, it is most likely that she was put in an armchair where she died.

Obviously the multicoloured *Woman Wearing a Hat Seated in an Armchair* (cat. 79) seems merrier and the beribbonned hat gives her a triumphant look. She too is an effigy of Dora Maar and the viewer can follow in detail the making of the first of Picasso's colour prints. It is likely that the five copperplates were too heavily worked over for it to be printed. Even the most simplistic analysis of the mythology of dreams tells us that a woman in an armchair is also a woman in the arms of a man. Proust (yes, again!) quotes 'Aldous Huxley's uncle' on the case of a young woman who always refused to sit in the armchair offered to her because she was sure she saw in it an old gentleman. This is far from invalidating the reference to Picasso's mother. That enormous beribbonned hat too, is another allusion, another symbol…

In July 1939 there was a trip to Antibes and then a return journey to Paris for Vollard's burial. And the war: Royan, Paris, Royan, and at last the definitive homecoming to occupied Paris. It was also, as far as printmaking was concerned, a complete disaster. Lacourière's workshop was shut or barely functioning before 1942, as all the workmen had been called up and the painters had all gone off to find secure refuge. No work could be done and the Lacourières had retired to their country house of Chessy, occasionally coming back to Paris by canoe, bringing with them butter, meat and vegetables. And later the workshop was 'occupied' by Derain, whom Picasso disliked. Still, in 1942, he and Lacourière sorted out the copperplates stored in the workshop and decided to use the remaining paper with 'Picasso' or 'Vollard' watermarks to print about fifty impressions of some of the plates, together with about a hundred of the portraits of Dora Maar in colour. They will never be signed, numbered, or put on sale.

The death of Vollard, the artist's official print dealer was a real catastrophe; Picasso, after fighting with him like cat and dog, had grown to like and respect him. But what on earth had happened to the thousands of impressions of the 'Vollard Suite'? Picasso was very perturbed about this. Vollard's nephew sent him off to Fabiani who was silent or gave only the vaguest of replies. As for Lacourière, he knew nothing or very little. He still managed to bring the artist a 'suite' on small paper of 'working impressions'. Picasso was never to get any artist's proofs, apart from the sumptuous series on parchment pulled prior to Vollard's death and which was already in his possession.

With Vollard dead and Kahnweiler in hiding, other dealers tried to take over. For example, Fabiani turned up with Picasso's illustrations for the *Histoires naturelles* of Buffon[13] which he had bought from the Vollard estate. But it was the Galerie Leiris, of which Kahnweiler was the sleeping partner, which now planned for the future as far as the prints were concerned. Somebody had to replace Vollard. In 1943, Louise Leiris published two of the prints Lacourière had printed in 1942: *Combat dans l'arène* (*Fight in the Arena*) on the paper with 'Picasso' *and* 'Vollard' watermarks, and *The Woman with a Tambourine*, on Arches, priced at 3000 francs. In 1943 this was not an enormous sum of money, but 'decent folk' no longer had any.

And then, in 1943 and especially in 1944, Lacourière was not at all well. His young tubercular daughter had eloped and come back so ill that she died. Though that kind of thing did not alter Picasso's friendship with Lacourière, he was utterly unable to accept that the friends he saw frequently were unhappy, depressed, sad.

During the Occupation, Picasso made hardly any prints. One of them, however, *Paris, July 14th 1942* (cat. 90), can be cited mostly because of its reverential and conundrum-like atmosphere. Its cheerfulness is amazing to say the least. The artist must have worked on it to pass the time while some trial proofs of the old plates were being pulled, as he was not keen to take the Métro up to the Butte Montmartre.

If I call this composition's festive look amazing, it is because this was the darkest period during the occupation of Paris. The Germans were being victorious on all fronts. The persecution of Jews was taking on hideous proportions (the 'round-up of the Vel-d'Hiv' took place on 16 and 17 July). There was nothing to eat. Bombs. Everything was getting worse – but Picasso was feeling better.

Brassaï wrote that a proof of this fairly large zincplate was displayed somewhere in Picasso's studio in the rue des Grands-Augustins and that Sabartés had told him it was the beginning of *L'Homme au mouton* (*The Man with the Sheep*).[14] The man with the flowers will take the lamb out of the old lady's arms, he said, and will keep it. And, as a matter of fact, the first preparatory drawings for the major sculpture began on 15 July. Interestingly enough, the old lady originally carried a lamb as well as a baby which Picasso 'scraped out' as it was redundant.

It so happens that a pre-Civil War photograph exists of the entire family of Picasso in Barcelona.[15] One can see in it Picasso's mother, an old lady, very different from the one in the print, except for her shortness and her air of dignity. The group with children, young people, parents and so on (naturally without the food which the figures in the print carry, and minus the goat and the lamb) reminds us somehow of the small group standing in front of the man with the flowers. It is not that there is any direct reference (except perhaps the woman with the doves, who may be an allusion to his sister Lola seen with a hat on the right of the photograph),[16] but it has the same graphic rhythm.

Might it be that his mother, who liked only young children, entrusts this lamb, a symbol of life and hope, into the man's care, thus transforming him into the

Cat.45 **Flute Player and Sleeping Woman/ Flûtiste et dormeuse** 1933

Drypoint on copper, states I and XXXI (colour)

Cat. 46 **Flute Player and Sleeping Woman/ Flûtiste et dormeuse** 1933

Monotype on copper, both pulled from state XXXI

Marie-Thérèse Walter at the age of 13. Photograph taken 20 October 1922 at the Boettger Institution, Wiesbaden (Archives nationales, Paris)

Good Shepherd? Could it be – as the rest of his work seems to show – that Picasso has almost finished mourning for his mother, whether or not he really knew what he was doing.

This mother who wrote to him nearly every other day, or at least once a week, and who, when he first settled in Paris, reminded him, in one of her letters, of those nights in Barcelona when, after he had stopped roaming around in the streets and came back home, he would always go into her bedroom to say good night (or good morning) as if to efface by that last kiss all the goings-on of the previous night.

If our hypothesis is correct, it would mean that the man had finally made peace with his mother: a loving one, no doubt, but a trifle possessive and 'bossy'. In any

case, the artist's work becomes more detached, more like that of a spectator, and he himself becomes more cynical. Passion will no longer play any part in his existence.

1. Christian Zervos, *Pablo Picasso*, 33 vols, Paris 1932–78.
2. Gauguin's annotations: "… *cette étrange figure, cruelle énigme [qui] engendra Séraphitus-Séraphita*"; Balzac's story is entitled *Séraphîta*.
3. "*Passe entre mes regards sans briser leur absence*", Paul Valéry, *Intérieur*.
4. Alfred de Musset, French poet and playwright (1810–57). Quotation from his play, *Le Chandelier*. "*Si vous croyez que je vais dire/Qui j'ose aimer/ Je ne saurais, pour un empire/ Vous la nommer*".
5. A great deal of ink has been spilled over the cult of Mithras, so popular with Romans, especially Roman soldiers, at the beginning of the Christian Era. There is no point in trying to relate Mithras to Picasso's work. For him a corrida was a corrida, that elaborate dance of death and love between the torero and the bull. Isn't it enough? Besides, the Mithraic symbolism was much more in fashion in England than in France, and that mainly between 1905 and the First World War. We can discard Mithras.
6. Jean-Baptiste Coquelin, called Molière (1622–73), French playwright. The quotation is from his play *Les Fourberies de Scapin.*. It is an expression well known to the French meaning "Why did he/she have to get involv ed in this business?'
7. Werner Spies in collaboration with Christine Piot, *Picasso, Das plastische Werk*, Stuttgart 1983.
8. On the relationship of the model to its representation, see Luigi Pirandello, *I Quaderni de Serafino Gubbio operatore*, 1925, in which the woman, who has a young painter as a lover, is 'wilder' and more sophisticated than Marie-Thérèse (but women do have feelings!). The author writes: "She obviously did not, because she could not, share it [the pleasure he had in caressing her body on a canvas]. Now, nothing is more irritating than to be excluded from the strong, obvious, and clear joy in front of us, the reason for which we are not able to discover or guess."
9. Maurice Merleau-Ponty (1908–61), French philosopher.
10. André Malraux, *La tête d'obsidienne*, Paris 1974, p. 118. Anecdotes and reported conversations should always be treated with caution, even if Malraux's imagination enabled him to extract the substance of the artist's words, which others disguise either to feed their theories or to flatter their own vanity. See also Proust, *Contre Sainte-Beuve*, Paris 1954 (collection 'Idées'), particularly p. 157.
11. Paul-André Lemoisne, *Degas et son oeuvre*, Paris 1946–49; reprinted New York and London 1984.
12. Malraux, *op. cit., ibidem*.
13. Georges Louis Leclerc comte de Buffon (1707–88), French naturalist and writer.
14. Brassaï, *Conversations avec Picasso*, Paris 1964, p. 137.
15. I found this photograph in the small catalogue, *J. Fin, graveur*, Galerie La Fenêtre, Paris 1989, p. 13.
16. Picasso's sister married a man named Vilato and the photograph comes from the Vilato archives.

*Bust of a woman (Marie-Thérèse)*, 1931

Cat.48 **Sculpture. Head of Marie-Thérèse/ Sculpture. Tête de Marie-Thérèse** 1933 Drypoint and scraper on copper, state I

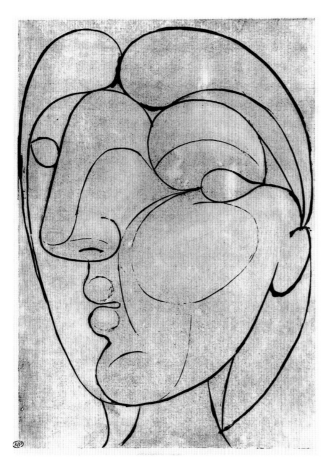

Cat. 48 **Sculpture. Head of Marie-Thérèse/ Sculpture. Tête de Marie-Thérèse**
1933 Monotype on copper, pulled from state IV

Cat.48 **Sculpture. Head of Marie-Thérèse/ Sculpture. Tête de Marie-Thérèse** 1933 Drypoint and scraper on copper, state V

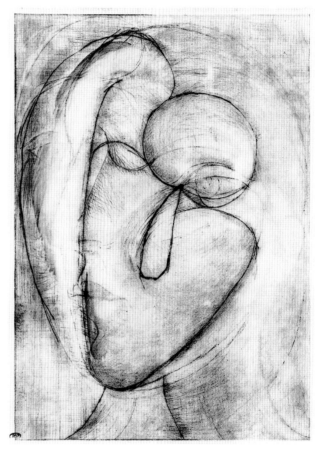

Cat. 48 **Sculpture. Head of Marie-Thérèse/ Sculpture. Tête de Marie-Thérèse** 1933 Drypoint and scraper on copper, state VI

Cat. 48 **Sculpture. Head of Marie-Thérèse/ Sculpture. Tête de Marie-Thérèse** 1933 Drypoint and scraper on copper, state VIII

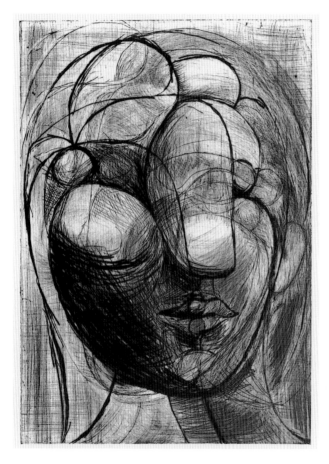

Cat. 48 **Sculpture. Head of Marie-Thérèse/ Sculpture. Tête de Marie-Thérèse** 1933  Drypoint and scraper on copper, state XX

Cat.49 **Sculpture. Head of Marie-Thérèse/ Sculpture. Tête de Marie-Thérèse** 1933  Monotype pulled from state XX

Cat. 50 **Sculptural Profile of Marie-Thérèse/ Profil sculptural de Marie-Thérèse** 1933 Etching and drypoint on copper, reworked
with lithographic crayon

Cat. 51 **Sculpture. Profile of Marie-Thérèse/ Sculpture. Profil de Marie-Thérèse** 1933

Before biting; inking and monotype made over ground stopped out with Marie-Thérèse's nail polish (enlarged)

# The hand, the manner

Many print collectors have only the vaguest notion of 'how it is done'. In a way, they may be right. What matters to them is the beauty of the picture (in the way children use the word when speaking of a 'picture book'), and they undoubtedly care about the quality of the impression. To a certain extent, this was also Picasso's point of view. His concern was the result, and he was ready to obtain it by any means, no matter how unorthodox. Although experts have tried for the past twenty years to determine exactly what methods an artist used to work his plates, it is not necessary to be a printmaker oneself to appreciate the end result.

There is no need to be obsessed by technique. Basically, it only makes a difference insofar as it adds to the meaning, character, beauty or to the ugliness, strangeness or apparent simplicity of a printed image. Even if a print is technically perfect, subtly handled after many long days of arduous labour, it can be devoid of interest if it displays nothing more than a technical exercise.

The old masters did everything themselves. Contemporary artists, however, tend to need constant technical assistance from a professional – an experienced printer – who regularly shows them how to obtain the effect they seek. Picasso's methods can be placed at a point midway between these two extremes. He never really learned printmaking. In other words, he never spent months in a print workshop practising under the supervision of a master printmaker. In the beginning, someone obviously showed him the rudiments, the tools and how to use them. Perhaps it was his Spanish friend Ricardo Canals, or the printer Delâtre's son, with the latter's wise old father providing additional advice. Most probably it was a combination of all three. Even though the elder Delâtre had stepped aside to let his son Eugène run the workshop, the young Picasso would

have been more receptive to the old man's advice. The only person who had ever taught him anything when he was a child was his own father. There was no need for long explanations, since Picasso was good with his hands and demonstrated a remarkable virtuosity. He began to experiment by himself, turning his back on the workshop except to complain about what he felt were intrusions (in the inking). After 1907 and until 1932, he managed to get along on his own, for example using copperplates that already had applied ground. To bite the plates, he called upon a professional, Fort, who was only a printer, not a printmaker. Nevertheless, when he felt the need, Picasso grabbed whatever was at hand – a piece of copper or zinc, often quite dirty. He laid the ground any which way and printed them himself without waiting another minute, because he was anxious to see 'what he had done'. By around 1907, he had acquired a small press.

Between the autumn of 1932 and the autumn of 1934, Picasso worked alone, in his own studio, with his small press, even though he had also purchased Fort's press. This was not installed in Boisgeloup until 23 April 1934. It was rarely used there, only a few proofs being pulled on it. The artist no longer had a printer. He learned the craft and made numerous experiments, heretical for a professional printmaker.

He began to work at Roger Lacourière's studio in Paris during the last months of 1934. Lacourière, who was a genius as far as printmaking was concerned, showed him various techniques, such as burin engraving, as well as several tricks of the trade. But he mostly placed 'elements' at Picasso's disposal (aquatint, 'sugar', etc.). Lacourière never interfered in his creative work, nor would Picasso have tolerated it. As if by accident, however, Lacourière would just happen by, glance over Picasso's shoulder while he was working,

Roger Lacourière in the workshop watching his reproduction of one of Picasso's watercolours (1942 or 1943). Private collection.

and casually make some useful remark, some suggestion ("why not try this or that?"). Nevertheless, during this period, Picasso began to abandon workshop tasks – that is to say, preparing the plate, laying the ground, biting the plate, pulling the proofs of the states (a state, which shows the different stages of the print, is a proof pulled in order to see what is happening before continuing the work), and the trial proofs. As a result, his own work went that much faster, which suited his inherent impatience, though he could not understand why all the workers wanted to go home in the evening, when he wanted to remain until midnight! It was forbidden to touch his work, to improve it, even to remove a spot. His possessiveness was equalled only by his impatience. It was as if a cook were perfectly content to let everyone else wash the pots and pans as he pressed forward with his concoction. Others could peel the vegetables, but their participation had to stop there. They must never touch the mixture bubbling on the fire.

To take this analogy even further, open any printmaking manual. It is just as discouraging as an old cookbook, dating from when the cook had three scullions, two scullery maids, etc. Even before preparing a seemingly easy dish, it was first necessary to cook half a calf, three chickens, and the like. Thanks to these 'anticipations', the making of the dish itself could begin, that is, if there were a mind-boggling quantity of tools

and ingredients at hand. In the same way, before even contemplating actually etching, an artist who wants to work by himself, without the participation of a specialized workshop, must first assure a slow and fastidious preparation. There are thousands of recipes to remember, thousands of precautions to take, before, during and after, in order to succeed in the operation without running the risk of ruining the work of the etching itself.

While he was obliged to accept the fact that there were rules, Picasso's very character would have made him reject them. First and foremost, he was very impatient. He was rapidly fed up with finicky preliminaries, whether they involved preparing a copperplate, or pulling a proof. He was, moreover, very violent. His burin, his etching needle, and his scraper are used with so much force that it seems as if he wanted to gouge right through the copper. Even in etching, his needle, instead of gliding smoothly in the ground, attacks the plate underneath. Nevertheless, Picasso succeeds in turning these handicaps into the something special that produces the personal style of his printed work. The conventional techniques, misused and mistreated, are forced to yield to the circumstances. Anything goes in order to give form to his conceptions.

On the other hand, when it was a question of a pure work of printmaking rather than some 'chemical' procedure, his stubbornness in obtaining what he sought was an asset (but perhaps it was also a way of calming his nerves, of pacifying the 'minotaur', a way of making the time go by while he waited, for example, for the paint to dry). He was capable, after 'preparing' with some thirty monotypes, of reworking a very small plate (*Flute Player and Sleeping Woman*; cat. 45) in the traditional way by 'adding on' to it, progressing through thirty-one states. Then, still not satisfied, he reworked the last state through 'destruction' in the form of some fifteen monotypes (cat. 46). This is only one example. The problem was that this method of working and reworking the copperplate wore it out to such an extent that only a small number of prints could be pulled from it. On other occasions, the artist created a simple,

Cat. 52 **Sculptor and Model with a Mirror/ Sculpteur et modèle se regardant dans un miroir calé sur un autoportrait sculpté** 1933 Etching on copper

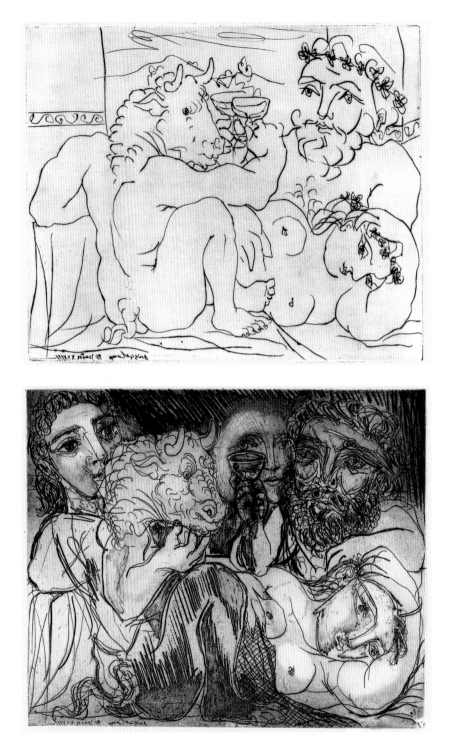

Cat. 55 **Marie-Thérèse Dreaming of Metamorphoses/ Marie-Thérèse rêvant de métamorphoses: elle-même et le sculpteur buvant avec un jeune acteur grec jouant le rôle du minotaure** 1933 (I) and end of 1934  Drypoint, etching, scraper and burin on copper, states I and III/IV

relatively empty, freehand image, that was perfect the first time around.

Picasso was both inventive and good with his hands. He often used whatever he came across, 'found', or met up with. One of his printmaker/printers, Aldo Crommelynck, an extremely knowledgeable craftsman, admits that sometimes he himself cannot figure out what Picasso could have done to his plate in order to obtain his results. He often gives the impression of having decided either to make the plate work or to work it to death. Generally it worked, sometimes not.

Picasso had two obsessions concerning printmaking. First he wanted to 'paint' in order to obtain printed surfaces. Basically he sought to create the effect of washes. Around 1924–25 he had several inconclusive experiences. Then in 1934 Lacourière provided him with the means to this end by introducing him to the technique of aquatint in all its forms. It was Lacourière who took care of the meticulous preparations that aquatint requires.

His second driving desire was to be able to trace 'freehand' lines in a single gesture without raising his hand – lines that followed the outline of an entire figure, or even a group of figures. Easy to do with a pencil, still possible in an etching, this becomes impossible with drypoint or in a burin engraving. He accomplished his desire in 1907, in the hardest and most difficult form, with the woodcuts of the eagle and the chick for Apollinaire's *Bestiaire* (cat. 9, 10). He tried out this idea once again in 1924–25, with etchings related to the ballet *Mercure*. But it must certainly have felt like struggling against all odds to be able to make more or less continual lines in white against the black background of an aquatint, a thing he managed to do in 1970.[1]

Technique is nothing more than a means. It is possible for several easily etched lines to produce a much more beautiful result than that of a plate which an artist has slaved over for long hours or days. Nevertheless, in order to study Picasso as a printmaker it is necessary to know a bit about how a print is created, or at least how a print is *supposed* to be created. This makes it possible to appreciate what is intrinsically his

own in his work.

Therefore a brief explanation of the techniques Picasso used is in order. The sequence does not follow their historical development but rather the chronology of the artist's experimentation.

Picasso began with etching (1899, then 1901 and 1904). Etching is an intaglio technique: that is to say, the incised part rather than the surface holds the ink which prints onto the paper. When the preparation and the biting of the copperplate are carried out by a craftsman, etching is the easiest method of all. The point or needle effortlessly glides over the ground, enabling the artist to trace his line with a great deal of freedom. Ever since the second half of the nineteenth century, etching has had the reputation of being the most successful medium for prints made by painters (as opposed to prints made by professional printmakers).[2]

The ease in making an etching comes from the fact that it is the acid, rather than a tool, which incises the metal. Where the copperplate is exposed by the etching needle, it is attacked – bitten – by the acid. The most delicate part is in the preparation of the copper (or the zinc) plate, its polishing, its cleaning and the laying of the ground. Normal etching ground, which is supplied in a solid ball, goes on hot and must be spread in a thin, even layer with a firm cloth dabber. There are also fluid grounds, but they must be used as soon as they are put on, since they flake when they become too dry. Usually, in order to see how the work is progressing, the surface is blackened with smoke so that the etching needle will leave a metal-coloured trace. Corrections can be made by retouching the surface with fluid ground. If the artist is more or less satisfied with his work, the hard part (if he is doing it himself) of biting the plate comes next. Held by tongs, the plate is plunged into a bath containing acid and water. The higher the percentage of acid, the faster the process, but it is important to be very careful, since every half-minute counts. In order to bite zinc plates, it is necessary to use nitric acid, which can also be used, though less effectively, for copperplates. Nitric acid has many major drawbacks, not the least of which are the fumes which are harmful to the lungs when inhaled. Lacourière, who never took the necessary precautions, fell prey to this professional hazard. Moreover, nitric acid boils in the incised lines, forming bubbles. In order to get rid of these, the plate must either be constantly rocked to and fro or stroked with a goose feather. Without this precaution, the bubbles are apt to 'decorate' the incised lines with small circles. Copperplates are traditionally bitten with ferric chloride, which does not boil. While it can cause the skin to become very dry, it does not harm it in any other way and it does not give off any fumes. Therefore, it is a much less dangerous acid. However, it works much more slowly and cannot be used to bite zinc plates.

As soon as the printer judges or predicts that the plate is sufficiently bitten, he must rinse it in running water. In this way, chance plays a role in etching. For the non-professional it is magic, as the etching is created by the biting. Nothing, or at least very little, is known until the first proof is pulled. It is nevertheless possible to sense that certain incised lines are too deep, or too tightly grouped together, just there, in that spot, where a bit of reflected light is necessary. So the scraper is taken in hand to scrape, or the burnisher to burnish. That is exactly what Picasso did in the first state of *The Frugal Repast* (cat. 2), which proves that he was capable of judging right off the bat, an even more amazing feat than the virtuosity of his first real etching. This brings us to a discussion of inking and printing, even if the artist did not print his own proofs.

The pulling of a proof is basically the same for all the intaglio techniques. In principle, the ground is removed from the plate, which is cleaned and polished, and then inked. The ink employed is oily and is applied with a soft leather pad or with muslin to make it penetrate thoroughly below the surface, into the incised lines. The plate is then wiped clean, first with a stiff cloth called tarlatan, then with the palm of the hand. When the surface is shiny clean, the plate can be pulled. It is placed on the bed of the press, where it is covered with a damp sheet of unsized paper limp as a piece of cloth. For protection, all of this is swaddled with pieces of felt called *langes* ('blankets') to cushion the plate and

distribute the pressure evenly. All that remains to be done is to put the press in motion and then to dry the proof, which is usually placed flat between paper blotters. The edge of the copperplate leaves an indentation around the proof: this is the plate mark. Obviously, the image is reversed. It all sounds simple, and of course it is, for a trained professional. Generally speaking, Picasso did rather well with small plates, though his inking was frequently too thin, and sometimes the paper tore or crumpled. First and foremost, what he wanted was to see – he cared little about the beauty of the proof.

A few more words about inking – the type described above, in which the plate is thoroughly wiped so that the ink remains only in the incised lines, is natural or straight inking, '*nature*'. There is another type called '*retroussé*' (or custom wiping), which makes the incised line thicker and runnier, leaving a tone on the surface. To achieve this effect, the plate is diagonally wiped with muslin so that the ink slightly overflows the incised lines. This 'custom wiping' of the plate can also be varied, leaving a tone on certain parts of the plate and polishing other places to create effects of light that, in fact, do not exist. The ink can also be worked with a rag to make shadows, or even 'things' that do not exist in the etched plate itself. This is called a print 'with effects' or, in workshop slang, to '*saucer*' (sauce) a proof. Picasso sometimes used such tricks to make his monotypes, but for his etchings he always asked his printers to pull the proofs '*nature*', which is to say 'straight'. Picasso could play around with what he had made. The printer, however, was not supposed to leave any mark or interpretation of his own. Even sixty years after he had worked with Delâtre on the plates of *The Saltimbanques*, Picasso still vituperated about the Delâtre workshop to Aldo Crommelynck. He still protested that the artists had not been allowed in the room where the proofs were pulled. The Delâtre workshop was famous for its 'saucing'. Later, when he decided in 1942 to have Lacourière print his 1939 *The Woman with a Tambourine* (cat. 78), he agreed (the *bon à tirer* corroborates it) to let the edition be printed in

Cat. 56 **Minotaur and Sleeping Woman/ Minotaure caressant du mufle la main d'une dormeuse** 1933 and 1934  Drypoint on copper

Cat. 57 **Copulation/ Accouplement. II** 1933

Etching and drypoint on copper, states I and IV

such a way that what was lacking in the background aquatint would be hidden, in order to make the background even and velvety. This was because what was being corrected was not his own mistake, but rather the fault of the workshop. The dusting box and the vat had been too small for the plate to fit in all at once. This exception to the rule was unique.

As soon as Picasso undertook to make prints by himself in his own studio, etching began to play tricks on him. Fluid grounds that were too dry began to flake. Incised lines developed offshoots reminiscent of a budding willow (an accident that he turned into a windfall for the 'little bathers' around the plate for Tristan Tzara's *Antitête*, 1932; cat. 42A). Elsewhere grounds cracked and acid seeping underneath made spots. As soon as he found Lacourière, he left such manipulations to the workshop. The rest took care of itself.

Picasso tried drypoint, a different intaglio technique, at the beginning of 1905. Here too the incised line is filled with ink and printed. However, the printmaker himself must cut into the metal freehand with a needle. Held between the fingers, like a pencil, the drypoint needle cuts into the metal, more or less deeply, depending on the pressure applied. This scoring action raises a small shaving of metal called burr on each side of the line. The burr which remains on the plate is highly appreciated by collectors since it is fragile and quickly wears down, after the printing of just a few proofs. Burrs render the inking more difficult since, if they are to be visible, the ink must not run, and also the ridges scrape the hands.

Of course, the drypoint does not glide so freely as for an etching where it only has to scratch through the ground. The metal is hard and resists. In some way or other, the composition is bound to embody this tension, this strain. There is inevitably something more violent, more lively, in a drypoint. Moreover, these ragged ridges (in Rembrandt's work, for example) produce admirable velvety shadows. The tiers of strong, violent strokes succeed in creating a dramatic effect unequalled by any other technique (see the fourth state of Rembrandt's *Three Crosses*). The ink that gets stuck in the burr does not print the same tone of black as the ink that is left on the paper by the etched line. Only around 1934 does Picasso seem to have begun to take an interest in Rembrandt's 'blacks'. He wanted to try to obtain them by different technical means, but, if the truth be told, he never succeeded.

Here, once again, Picasso did not work in the same way as anyone else. Just as he would not allow his proofs to be 'custom wiped' by someone else, he did not seem to have considered the burrs as part of his own personal work. They must have seemed to add something that was not his own. In one of his first drypoints, *Tête de femme de profil* (Head of a Woman in Profile; G/B 7), he apparently wants only neat, clean lines. He removes the burr and continues scraping. In the second state, he uses his scraper to model the face of his woman over a background of incised lines. When he adds a thick lock of hair, in the style of Paul Helleu, he immediately removes the burr from his incised lines.

The most important advantage that drypoint had for him was that the greater difficulty in handling the drypoint needle on the metal served to curb the facility of his hand for drawing. Somewhere Vasari spoke of a painter who considered the lack of effort as something harmful to the discipline, the firmness and the perfection of drawing. This painter said that in order to get rid of too much facility, it is necessary to practice drawing with the left hand. In the same way, the drawings from the last two years of Paul Klee's life have something fascinating derived from the difficulties caused by his physical disability.

Even slower and physically more strenuous is making a woodcut, the oldest printmaking medium. In the West, it was used for printing fabric patterns; in China and Japan, it was known as early as the ninth century. Already used on vellum and parchment, its practice spread through the West with the appearance of paper. The medium was revived towards the end of the nineteenth century. Picasso, after a trial experience (probably pyrogravure) around 1900 (*Torero Seen from the Back*; cat. 1), tackled woodcuts in 1906. Not for very long, though, since he preferred copper to anything else.

Cat. 58 **Rembrandt with Marie-Thérèse as His Model/ Rembrandt à la palette avec Marie-Thérèse comme modèle** 1934

Etching, drypoint and scraper on copper, states I and VII

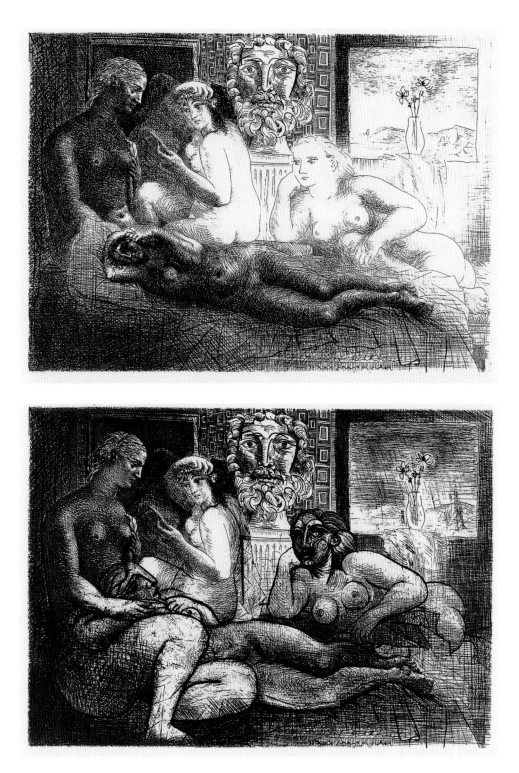

Cat. 59 **Women Together with a Sculpture-Voyeur (after Ingres)/ Femmes entres elles, avec voyeur sculpté (d'après le**
***Bain Turc*) 1934 and late 1934  Etching, scraper and burin on copper, states I and V

Cat. 62 **The Great Corrida with Female Matador/ La Grande Corrida, avec femme torero** 1934 Etching on copper

Cat. 64 **Two Masked Figures before a Harpy Perched on a Low Column/ *Chez la Pythie-Harpye*...** 1934 Aquatint on copper

With wood, it is the raised part, the unworked, untouched surface which prints. The cavity which is hollowed out, *'champlevée'*, chased, with a knife, a burin, or a gouge produces empty, light surfaces or lines on the paper of the proof. Picasso never used hard end-grain wood, but rather wood cut along the grain, in the same direction as a log split apart by an axe. But he did not have the necessary patience for this work. He used it mainly to obtain a 'drawing' in a blank against a coloured background. In this way he had only to cut away, to hollow out, what became 'the picture', just as Gauguin had done. Nevertheless, for the two small prints of *The Eagle* and *The Chick* (cat. 9,10), mentioned above, he limited himself to disengaging as best he could (and without all the meticulous subtleties

required) a 'continuous line' against a background that was cut away (which therefore had to be hollowed out with a penknife, but without cutting into the lines). Despite the great number of animals he had drawn in this spirit for Apollinaire's *Bestiaire* (and, as usual in these circumstances, to amuse Fernande's adopted daughter, Raymonde), Picasso abandoned the idea of illustrating his friend's book with woodcuts. It was much too discouraging. He inked his woodblocks with Indian ink, or with gouache, and pulled them by simply using the pressure of his hand.

Towards the end of 1905 Picasso also tried his hand at making monotypes. This technique can be situated halfway between painting or wash drawing and printmaking. It is simply a matter of 'painting' with

Cat. 65 **Marie-Thérèse as an Idol and Three Bearded Greeks/ Marie-Thérèse en idole et trois Grecs barbus**

1934  Sugar lift aquatint, scraper, burin and etching on copper, states I and VI

Cat. 66 **Sheet of Studies: Seated Nude and Head of a Bearded Man**/ Feuille d'études: Barbu et femme assise de dos

1934 Etching on screened celluloid (enlarged)

oily or greasy ink – at least in principle, but Picasso used Indian ink and gouache, applied with a brush or a cloth on any flat surface: copper, glass, but also, in his case, paper or canvas. This is pressed by hand, or by using a press, against a sheet of paper. The first result is the reversal of the image, but then the pressure, especially if it is done with a press, modifies the character of the material used, as well as the limits of the lines and the surfaces. Greasy ink, for example, can result in a quantity of small dots or droplets.

In fact, it is difficult to explain the beauty of certain monotypes, their mystery, their 'reality', and the differences they present, for example, with an identical ink wash. The unsurpassed master of this medium is, of course, Degas. It is impossible to know whether Picasso at this early stage could have seen certain monotypes by this painter. One of Degas's 'black monotypes' – *i.e.* those showing women at their toilet, worked with cloth *en réserve* (using negative space) – was reproduced in a Vollard album in 1914. Perhaps at the time of the Degas sales in 1918–19 at the Galerie Georges Petit, Picasso might have had the opportunity of leafing through a portfolio containing these works that the public discovered much later. Vollard owned a number of them. Others, particularly the 'black monotypes' (for example, the superb *Cheminée*, Cachin 167[3]), were exhibited by Georges Petit in 1924. Many of these monotypes were included in the Orangerie exhibition in 1937. These marvellous works do not seem to have had any sort of influence on Picasso's technique or manner, at least not as far as his own monotypes are concerned. But the proof, heightened in the press, of the third state of *Two Women and a Nude Model* (cat. 18) introduces a doubt. Moreover, the way in which Picasso transformed his *The Woman with a Tambourine* in its fourth state (cat. 78) can only be a transposition (using a different technique) of the results that Degas achieved by wiping with a cloth.

If, up to 1931, Picasso's monotypes are independent works, during several months in 1933 he frenetically employed this technique in order to prepare compositions for prints. He even used it to extend, by

totally transforming it, a drypoint like *Flute Player and Sleeping Woman* (cat. 45, 46). This plate had been worked on so much that it had become impossible to labour at it any more.

His most successful, most mysterious, monotype is definitely the *Marie-Thérèse in Profile* (cat. 39). It was not worked by wiping. A tarlatan cloth posed on the surface produced the velvety tones, the surface quality and the magic that the others do not have.

In 1915, for the first time, Picasso took up the burin, which is the oldest tool of intaglio engraving. This professional engraver's tool is very difficult to manipulate, at least when used according to the rules. To understand this, a glance at *Melencholia* I by Dürer, the uncontested master, is sufficient. The blade of a burin has a large handle which fits into the palm of the hand. The hard metal blade, which is beveled into either a square, triangular or lozenge shape, must be forced into the metal plate at the necessary angle in order to push out a fine shaving, producing a furrow that is deep or shallow, wide or narrow, according to the pressure exerted. The muscles of the palm propel the burin. Fingers merely serve to direct the tool. The burin always cuts straight in front of itself, like a plough; therefore it is the plate that must be turned. It is traditionally placed on a small sand-filled cushion, and the left hand is used to turn the plate. Both sides of the grooves are smoothed out so that the line obtained on the paper is perfectly clean. The line begins abruptly and ends in a point. Goldsmiths use exactly the same method to inlay metal, except that they fill in the incised lines with gold or enamel.

For his first work using a burin (G/B 51), Picasso struggled through eight states to arrive at a result that was vibrant, violent and monumental, despite its small size. Needless to say, he turned as little as possible, and rather badly. But it can also be said that if he used his tool in this way, it was because he was making a Cubist engraving. Despite a certain clumsiness, he obtained a much more lively result than he would have achieved with another tool. However, burin engraving was really much too painstaking a technique for him. Before any real 'apprenticeship', he would all alone, at Boisgeloup, redo little by little, step by step, over eleven or twelve states of the 'drawing' already made with a drypoint (cat. 61) on the plate of his large *Minotaure aveugle* (*Blind Minotaur*, G/B 434). Each 'step' was verified on Fort's press, newly installed at Boisgeloup, by using another bigger copperplate to 'swaddle' his plate. There, too, he turned as little as possible, but he was trying! It was only several months later, under Lacourière's wing, that he would, almost like a child learning to form the strokes of letters with a quill, make apple-peel spirals on the faces of the 'women among themselves' on a plate that he had begun in March 1934, but which he did not return to until the end of the year (*Women Together with a Sculpture-Voyeur*; cat. 59). It worked: the burin was willing to turn. But burin engraving was too boring, and afterwards he mainly used it for making corrections. He did not dabble in subtleties with this tool. His furrows were very deep, beginning with a sort of blob, generally going off in an almost straight line, and ending in a point. He attacked the plate with so much ardour that it is easy to believe that he wanted literally to pierce right through the copperplate. In 1936, Lacourière teased him in a letter, saying that he had bought four new burins – followed by three exclamation marks. He added, "If my dear father were still alive, he would predict my bankruptcy, since in his day a set of burins lasted nearly a lifetime" – an obvious allusion to the way Picasso treated the poor burins. For Picasso the burin, far from being the tool used by Dürer, was 'the instrument of emotion'.

The question of Picasso's violence has been raised. Even though it is not in itself a technique, his use of the scraper must be mentioned. It was not four, but rather four dozen, scrapers that Lacourière probably had to buy!

A scraper is a tool with a curved, sharp-edged triangular shaped blade that ends in a point. As its name indicates, it is used to scrape the plate with successive shaving to 'erase' grooves, to model, to take away surfaces, to tone down aquatint, etc. Normally it is handled gently and either it returns a relatively smooth surface to the copperplate (although rougher than before) or, for example, on aquatint it produces a wide, light, even line. Picasso's use of the scraper is exceptional. Handled with extreme vigour, his scraper skids (it is tempting to say, while groaning) and leaves a sort of wavelet all along its path. The surface of the plate takes on a tortured aspect which produces a strong tone. This is that much the more irregular since Picasso's scraper, always chipped, never sharpened, claws at the copperplate like some sort of gardening tool. Picasso said that Rembrandt too scraped away like a madman (see his *Ecce Homo*), and that he really could not see why anyone would criticize these tones, and that they were perfect just as they were. It must be said that there is a definite difference between Rembrandt's scraper and Picasso's. When the grooves were very deep (see, for example, *Sculpture. Head of Marie-Thérèse*; cat. 48), in conventional terms the result is bizarre. The furrows that were removed hardly disappear and the scraper leaves its trace everywhere. Picasso also used the scraper like an engraving tool, a sort of wide, cutting drypoint needle. The resulting furrows can be described as having been made 'directly by the scraper'. In his hands the scraper becomes a spontaneous, inventive, and furious tool, a sort of 'Spanish bull'.

Sporadically, in 1914–15, Picasso tackled aquatint, which he would return to, with Lacourière's assistance, towards the end of 1934. His first work in aquatint, *Man with a Pipe* (cat. 17), can be, in fact, more accurately described as a work made with the scraper (with the addition of etching and drypoint). He most probably found a small piece of zinc already grained and bitten, perhaps in Delâtre's workshop. Or perhaps he had the printer do this work for him, since he did not possess the tools necessary for the preparation of the plate. This required a professional.

Picasso handled this tiny plate like a mezzotint. A word must be said about this technique that he would often use later. Originally, using a rocker (a tool which resembles a kitchen chopper, 'armed' with small points), the plate is covered with a quantity of tightly cross-hatched grooves and small hollows which retain the ink and, to the naked eye, produce a uniform background in the colour of the ink. Then with the scraper or the burnisher, the subject is traced in negative, modeled by the degree of force or delicacy used to scrape or crush the metal. The subject therefore appears in light tones against a dark background. As far as the preparation of the plate is concerned, aquatint is much more rapid than the rocker used in mezzotint, but the result is not necessarily as subtle.

Aquatint, which derives from etching, furnishes the means for 'painting'. It produces dark surfaces of ink, and not just lines. For the ink to stay on the copperplate when it is wiped, so that under the press it can be deposited onto the damp paper, it must be tucked away in grooves that are sufficiently thin to contain and retain it. If you try to paint on the surface with the acid, if having formed the areas to be protected from the acid with a varnish of some kind, you then plunge the otherwise unworked copperplate into the acid, there will be nothing to retain the ink. The surface will be slightly lowered, and with a slightly grainy zinc plate the relief and the hollows will be increased, but except for a special inking, only a few moderately satisfactory proofs can be pulled. Therefore, the plate must be covered with a quantity of little valleys separated by tiny plateaux. Only then will the ink remain in the hollows. It is their multiplicity that succeeds in giving the impression to the naked eye that the surface is continuously inked. Seen through a magnifying glass, the true structure of the surface appears, with its sinuous network of small lines, dotted with more or less dense white spots, irregularly and randomly placed.

The technique of aquatint dates from the second half of the seventeenth century, but was not commonly used until a century later. The ongoing modern process, which was used for Picasso by Lacourière, consists in covering a copperplate, as regularly as possible, with resin dust. Each of the little grains, which are made to adhere to the copper by heating the underside of the plate, prevents the acid from attacking. However, the acid does bite the bare metal around the grains. The finer the grain, the more velvety is the black obtained.

In order to achieve a truly black surface, the plate can be dusted and bitten twice, once with fairly large grains, once with very fine grains. Experts argue about which of the two procedures should come first.

Goya is incontestably the master of aquatint. He did everything himself, and there are differing opinions as to what he did. In Picasso's time, print workshops made use of a dusting box. It is a box hermetically sealed except for the side where the plate is introduced. To simplify, let us say that inside is placed a small pile of resin, of grains, of resinous dust. A bellows or a fan makes this resin fly up until it falls down and comes to rest on the plate. Then the plate is carefully removed and placed on a heater, which by melting the resin glues down this dust which, just a moment before, would have been disturbed by the slightest puff of air. Inside the box, the heaviest grains fall first, then come the lighter, finer grains. This is the way that the graining can be varied. Lacourière carried out all these steps for Picasso, who never tried it himself.

Either the whole plate can be grained (then a ground can be laid on the surfaces destined to become clear) or the places that should remain intact are stopped out, and the rest is grained. Lines which are too wide can also be grained, since without this precaution they would not hold ink (but that is a matter for the workshop 'cuisine'). Afterwards the only thing left to do is to bite the plate.

Before the end of 1934, Picasso indulged in some more or less unusual experiments in order to obtain a dark background on a plate. Around 1924–25, he tried to intensify the graininess of a zinc plate by biting it with nitric acid around a grounded area (in his *Carnet de Zincs*; cat. 22, 30, 31, 33). At the beginning of 1933, he fiddled with suet or something like it, dabbling it lightly with a stick rolled in cotton, so that the acid went more or less through the suet. Around the same time, he used nail polish to stop out and left his copperplate in the acid for so long that it produced a tone (*Sculpture. Profile of Marie-Thérèse*; cat. 51). In November 1933 he indulged himself in a sort of alchemy, either laying his ground with a wad of newspaper, which left manipulated stopped-out areas, or by smearing a porous product with almost no coating power (diluted waxes, soot, greasy ink, or whatever). See, for example, *Copulation, II* (cat. 57), in which the 'drawing' is made *en réserve* with lithographic crayon. All these experiments suggest that Picasso really needed the aquatint technique that Lacourière provided him with at the end of 1934.

After mid-November of that year Lacourière began to show Picasso classical aquatint. One time it was simply a question of shading the second state of the *Garçon pensif veillant une dormeuse* (*Thoughtful Boy Watching over a Sleeping Woman*, G/B 440), since the lines the artist had made were too wide and tightly grouped to hold the ink. Another time it was to fabricate something more elaborate, a subject traced with varnish, grained, and then bitten by hand by the artist. The biting is done with a brush, the artist trying to predict what may happen, since nothing is visible. The tones produced are darker or lighter according to the amount of biting; therefore, with the intervention of the artist's hand, there is a much subtler background (see *Two Masked Figures before a Harpy Perched on a Low Column*; cat. 64). At the end of November, Picasso took on his first sugar aquatint (first state of Marie-Thérèse as an idol on *Sheet of Studies*; cat. 65) before returning during the month of December to the technique close to mezzotint that he had used in 1914–15.

Given the use Picasso made of the sugar aquatint and the mastery he achieved in its manipulation, using all sorts of extravagant methods, it seems appropriate to provide an explanation. For the artist, it was very simple. He painted on his copperplate with a more or less liquid sugar syrup, tinted with ink. The sole purpose of the ink is to render the operation visible. Once this 'paint' was dry, the more meticulous work of the printer began. The plate was covered with a light ground, and when this ground was quite dry, the whole thing was plunged into water. The water melted the sugar, which made the ground permeable where the sugar had been applied, thus ungluing and lifting ground. The copperplate laid bare corresponds to the 'drawing' made by the artist; the rest of the plate remains stopped by the ground. The plate is grained; it is bitten. When printed, the artist's wash comes out in black against a virgin background. A uniform tone is obtained which can then be attenuated and modeled with a scraper, or with a burnisher, or redone in the same way to obtain half-tones. Obviously there are a great many subtleties which totally transform the stencil-like aspect of the basic technique.

The interest of this technique is that it provides a way of 'painting'. In the post-Second World War period, when Lacourière was ill, Picasso tried to use lithography in the same way. However, as soon as he had succeeded in completely mastering the lithographic process, it seems to have bored him. He preferred copperplates and aquatint.

In 1939, aquatint would enable him to venture into colour. But this did not last very long. Much later, in Mougins in the years 1965–70, Picasso said one day to Aldo Crommelynck that he was 'afraid' of colour printing. The word is strong, nevertheless he is the one who used it while talking shop, rather than while uttering truisms and paradoxes for public consumption. Perhaps, since he had no control over the person who printed the impressions of a colour edition, Picasso felt an intrusion into his work, something like the 'saucing' of the proofs that had so annoyed him during his youth in Delâtre's workshop. And then, it is a known fact that, because it oxidizes, the copperplate does not render true colours. Of course, during his experiments, the artist worked on copper. Then, in order to print in colour, the copper was steelfaced. The colours were no longer the same as those he had chosen in the beginning. His work was escaping his control. In reality, it was black and white he liked.

Around 1923, on the final state of *Two Women and a Nude Model* (cat. 18), Picasso devoted himself to the excessively meticulous work of 'colouring' with the press, in six printings, beginning by pulling the plate in black, then inking '*à la poupée*' (in principle, a small pad of rags resembling a rag doll, but also just a rag or simply a finger), colour by colour, the parts that he

73

wanted in red, in blue, etc. At the beginning of 1933, there was a new experiment with colours (with gouache as well). The black was still printed first, but all the colours were applied with a rag and printed in a single passage (in the thirty-first state of *Flute Player and Sleeping Woman*; cat. 45).

According to Lacourière's bill, between 31 December 1934 and 1 January 1935, Picasso and Lacourière played a strange game with the mezzotint of *Blind Minotaur in the Night* (cat. 66). This time, with Lacourière's help, the inking is modern[4] and used according to the rules (first the colours, inked *à la poupée*, and then the black). But the result resembles a veritable chromo dating from the beginning of the century. The choice of colour can only be attributed to a bad mood which goes way beyond that caused by this night of so-called festivities, during which Picasso always worked. It must be said that this oddity, this 'chromo-litholeo-margarine fake' (an invention of Kipling's) is no worse than the edition of Goya's *Caprichos* in the Norton Simon Museum, which was coloured by hand, probably at the end of the nineteenth century.

The proof of *The Minotauromachy* (cat. 68), inked with coloured inks, has true, frank colours, instead of those wedding-cake colours. It was made *à la poupée* in a single passage, but is less shocking and without a doubt more pleasant. Nevertheless, the black and white proofs are much more beautiful and much more dramatic. Why did he make this experiment? It is difficult to say. Was it just for fun? Or did Picasso have in mind his dealer Vollard, knowing he was in love with colour?

At any rate, a colour print is a print conceived by the artist in terms of colour printing. It is not a black and white print, coloured by hand or under the press, as an afterthought. It ought to be possible to make an edition with each impression being more or less the same as the others. The sporadic experiments cited above could not be reproduced. It was only in 1939, between January and June, that Picasso had, according to Sabartés, a 'fantasy' for colour. He invaded Lacourière's workshop, upsetting all the workmen day after day over a period of months. It should also be pointed out that the workshop

provided him with a means of escape, escape from himself (his mother had died on 13 January), from 'his women', from his nephews (Barcelona had fallen at the end of January, and when two of his nephews turned up in Paris in February Picasso 'confided' them to Lacourière, so that they could learn the craft), and escape from the oppression of this period of international crisis. What could be better than Montmartre and meticulous work as yet unfamiliar to him that he could slave at, he and the workshop assistants who grained, and bit the plates, and printed the proofs, as the work progressed. Vollard and Sabartés[5] were toying with the idea of making 'the total book', basically an 'artist's book' in the current sense of the word. They wanted to reproduce Picasso's 'writing', with words crossed out, spelling mistakes, the layout of the page. He would add remarques in the margins (see *XXXIV. "El clarín se retuerce…"*; cat. 84), plates with large colour portraits of women, and, as tail-pieces and headings, a series of small plates of bathers, in black and white and in colour (cat. 80A–83, 85–87). Even the paper was chosen!

But it was too much work, and perhaps Picasso had a keen enough sense of judgment to appreciate his 'automatic writing' at its true worth (especially in his allusion to the *Don Quixote* that Sabartés was hoping for). In short, the project failed and it would have failed in any case because of the death of Vollard in July. Picasso would, however, return to the idea of facsimiles of his writing, marginal remarques and plates with portraits of women for his *Gongora*, but without colour and accompanied by a real text.

The problem was that Picasso wanted to obtain the tones of watercolour, the transparency, the lightness of watercolour (*dixit* Sabartés); but when the layers of ink were superimposed, the result was inevitably a little thick and heavy. Moreover, the artist wanted to work each plate (there is one plate for each colour) as he would a black and white aquatint, scraping and redoing endlessly. At least in the beginning, he used five copperplates and five colours where four would have been enough, in the *Woman Wearing a Hat Seated in an*

*Armchair* (cat. 79) and in the *Tête de Femme No. 1* (Baer 648). In the middle of the twentieth century, when making a colour-aquatint one plate was used for each colour. The colours stabilized by steelfacing, were pulled (for an edition) one after the other. Between each printing, there was a pause to allow the ink to dry. The paper was again dampened for the following colour. As a rule, light colours were pulled first and black last.

But to work on the plates, the artist begins with the black or master plate, at least for the first state. What are called transfer proofs are pulled on a relatively non-absorbent paper which does not shrink, like strong Japan paper. Prussian blue ink is used, since it is especially strong and adherent. Freshly pulled, these proofs are transferred onto the number of copperplates necessary for establishing the colour plates. Generally, the plates which supply one or other of the colours are worked in order to produce flat tints (see the yellow in the *Woman Wearing a Hat Seated in an Armchair*).

But Picasso worked almost every colour plate as though it were the master plate, scraping, redoing the aquatint, reversing the order in which the colours were superimposed, changing his mind for the choice of the black plate. The *Woman Wearing a Hat Seated in an Armchair* was never printed, even though the copperplates had been steelfaced for the last two proofs of superposition. However, the six heads of women were printed in 1942, in eighty or even a hundred examples. Up until his death, no one knew that this mountain of impressions was stacked in one of his storage spaces, and collectors thought that there were only a few proofs of each print. Why? A great deal of Montval paper, watermarked Picasso or Vollard, had been left in the workshop. It was a good paper, it was wartime, therefore it was used. Undoubtedly Picasso feared the rapacity of Fabiani who had bought up Vollard's stock. Later on, too much time had passed and he was thinking about other things. Moreover, he apparently did not like these prints. He had signed, on the verso, several superpositions of the *Tête de Femme No. 3* (Baer 651), perhaps in order to demonstrate that he was the one who had chosen and mixed the inks and that he

considered those proofs to be his. As for the others, even if he had given his approval for the colours, the results were the work of someone else.

While the majority of the works exhibited here are trial proofs, it is perhaps appropriate to explain about steelfacing. Copper is a soft metal. In order to print (and Kahnweiler or Vollard would want one hundred to three hundred impressions), it was necessary to reinforce the copperplate, to steelface it. That means that the copperplate is covered with a film of steel by electrolysis. Picasso had had problems with the steelfacing of his *Saltimbanques*, and he was very distrustful of this procedure. But as far as colour plates are concerned, they must be steelfaced in order to stabilize the colours since, by provoking oxidation, copper transforms the tones.

It was only later, and in relation to aquatint (since it is difficult to obtain a 'straight' impression without steelfacing the copperplate), that Lacourière, at the beginning of the '50s, then – especially from 1963 on – Aldo and Piero Crommelynck, were able to persuade Picasso that this technique had now much improved. They also pointed out to him that the accidents which had occurred to the *Saltimbanques* were mostly due to the fact that the zinc had to be copperfaced before being steelfaced. He was now rich enough to use only copper. In short, steelfacing was no longer risky, and could provide a guarantee of a normal and '*nature*' printing.

Beginning in 1966, Picasso no longer gave true *bons à tirer*, since it was understood that printings would only be '*nature*', without any interpretation on the printers' part. He merely signed one of the impressions in the pile already printed, adding '*Bon à tirer*' as a gift to his printers.

1. When he unearthed a small tool which had a funnel that could be filled with fluid ground to 'draw' in the negative on an aquatint.
2. The leading expert on 19th-century prints, Beraldi, more or less says that anyone can make an etching, like playing the piano!
3. Jean Adhémar and Françoise Cachin, *Edgar Degas, Gravures et Monotypes*, Paris 1973.
4. See *Anatomie de la Couleur*, Paris 1996.
5. See Sabartés, *Picasso, Portraits et souvenirs*, Paris 1996, pp. 206–11 (first ed. Paris 1946, pp. 169–73).

Cat. 60 **Female matador. Last Kiss?/ Femme Torero. Dernier baiser?** 1934 Etching on copper

Cat. 67 **Blind Minotaur in the Night/ Minotaure aveugle guidé par Marie-Thérèse au pigeon dans une nuit étoilée** 1934–35 Aquatint, scraper, drypoint and burin on copper, state IV printed in colour

Cat. 68 **The Minotauromachy/ La Minotauromachie** 1935 Etching, scraper and burin on copper, state I

Cat. 68 **The Minotauromachy/ La Minotauromachie** 1935  Etching, scraper and burin on copper, state II

Cat. 68 **The Minotauromachy/ La Minotauromachie** 1935  Etching, scraper and burin on copper, state III

Cat. 68 **The Minotauromachy/ La Minotauromachie**  1935  Etching, scraper and burin on copper, state IV

Cat. 68 **The Minotauromachy/ La Minotauromachie** 1935 Etching, scraper and burin on copper, state V (private collection)

Cat. 68 **The Minotauromachy/ La Minotauromachie** 1935 Etching, scraper and burin on copper, state VI

Cat. 68 **The Minotauromachy/ La Minotauromachie** 1935 Etching, scraper and burin on copper, state VII

Cat. 68 **The Minotauromachy/ La Minotauromachie** 1935 Etching, scraper and burin on copper, state VII printed in colour

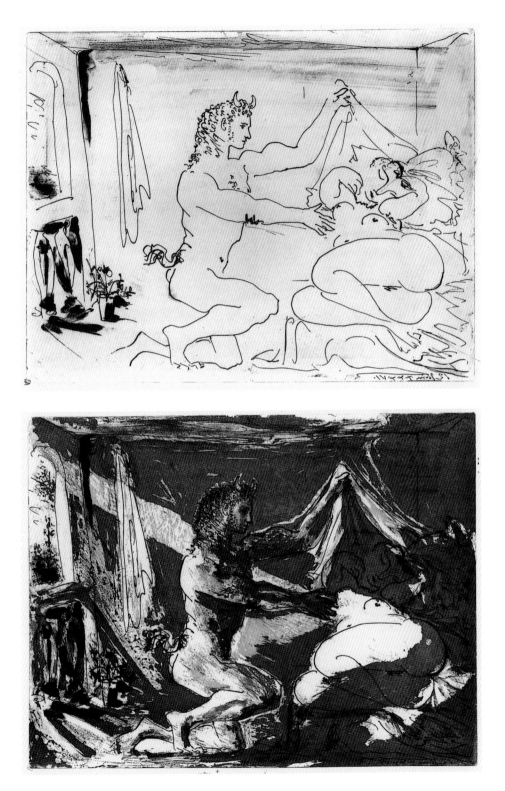

Cat. 69 **Faun Unveiling a Sleeping Woman/ Faune dévoilant une dormeuse** 1936

Aquatint, scraper and burin on copper, states I and III

Cat 69 **Faun Unveiling a Sleeping Woman/ Faune dévoilant und dormeuse** 1936  Aquatint, scraper and burin on copper, state VI

Rembrandt, *Jupiter and Antiope*, 1659

(Bibliothèque nationale de France, Paris)

Cat. 71 **Weeping Woman, I/ La Femme qui pleure. I** 1937 Drypoint, aquatint, etching and scraper on copper, states I and II

Cat. 71 **Weeping Woman, I/ La Femme qui pleure. I** 1937 Drypoint, aquatint, etching and scraper on copper, states III and IV

Cat. 71 **Weeping Woman, I/ La Femme qui pleure. I** 1937 Drypoint, aquatint, etching and scraper on copper, states V and VI

Cat. 71 **Weeping Woman, I/ La Femme qui pleure. I** 1937 Drypoint, aquatint, etching and scraper on copper, state VII

Cat. 72 **Weeping Woman, III/ La Femme qui pleure. III** 1937

Drypoint and aquatint on copper

Cat. 73 **Weeping Woman, IV/ La Femme qui pleure. IV** 1937

Drypoint on copper

Cat. 75 **Dora Maar, II/ Portrait de Dora Maar. II** 1937 Monotype on copper, with collage of flowers

Cat. 77 **Bust of a Seated Woman/ Buste de femme à la chaise** (Plate for
Breton's *Anthologie de l'humour noir*) 1938 Etching, aquatint, scraper and
burin on copper, state I

Cat. 77 **Bust of a Seated Woman/ Buste de femme à la chaise** (Plate for
Breton's *Anthologie de l'humour noir*) 1938 Etching, aquatint, scraper and
burin on copper, state X (private collection)

Cat. 78 **The Woman with a Tambourine/ La Femme au tambourin** 1939

Aquatint and scraper on copper, states I and II

Edgar Degas, *After the Bath*, 1883–84

(Private collection)

Cat. 78 **The Woman with a Tambourine/ La Femme au tambourin** 1939

Aquatint and scraper on copper, states III and IV

Nicolas Poussin, *Bacchanalia* (detail),
1632–33 (The Trustees of the National
Gallery, London)

Cat. 78 **The Woman with a Tambourine/ La Femme au tambourin** 1939

Aquatint and scraper on copper, state V

Cat. 79 **Woman Wearing a Hat Seated in an Armchair/ Femme au fauteuil
et au chapeau** 1939 Aquatint, scraper and burin, in five colours, on five separate
copperplates, states I (red) and VIII (black)

Cat. 79 **Woman Wearing a Hat Seated in an Armchair/ Femme au fauteuil et au chapeau** 1939 Aquatint, scraper and burin, in five colours, on five separate copperplates, states III (yellow) and VI (blue)

Cat. 79 **Woman Wearing a Hat Seated in an Armchair/ Femme au fauteuil et au chapeau** 1939 Aquatint, scraper and burin, in five colours, on five separate copperplates, definitive colour proof with all colours

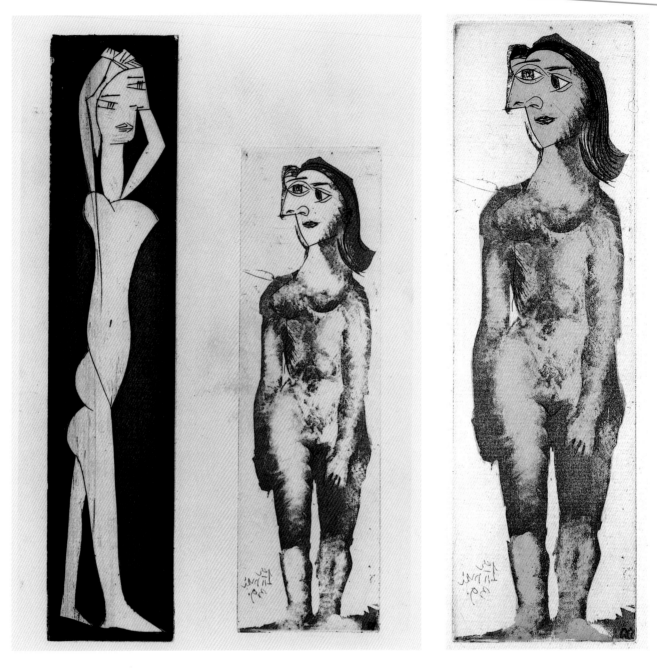

Cat. 80.(*Small prints for a book conceived by Vollard and Sabartés*)

3. **Walking Nude** and **Standing Nude, II/ Femme nue marchant** et **Nu debout. II**, state I, 1939
Burin and aquatint on two copperplates

2. **Standing Nude, II/ Nu debout. II** 1939 Burin and aquatint on two copperplates,
one used for colour, state II

100

5. (Poem, no. 34)/ "XXXIV. El clarin se retuerce..." 1939 Etching, scraper and burin on copper around a héliogravure reproduction of the artist's manuscript writing, state III

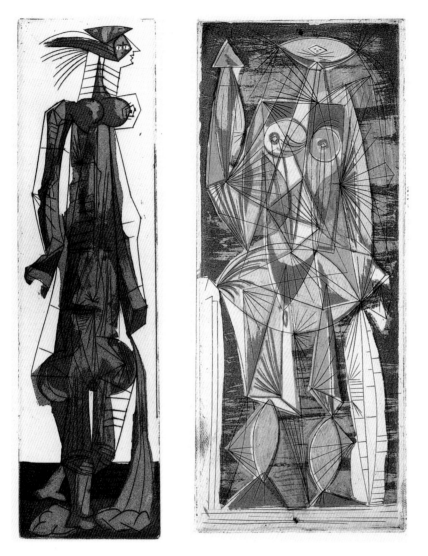

6. **Bather with a Towel, I/ Baigneuse à la serviette. I** 1939  Burin and aquatint on
copper, state III

7. **Bather with a Towel, III/ Baigneuse à la serviette. III** 1939  Burin and aquatint, in
four colours, on four copperplates

8. **Bather with a Ball and Towel/ Baigneuse à la balle et à la serviette** 1939  Aquatint,
scraper and burin on copper, state II/III

Cat. 81 **Woman in an Armchair/ Femme au fauteuil à balustres** 1939

Aquatint, scraper and burin on copper, states I and II

Cat. 81 **Woman in an Armchair/ Femme au fauteuil à balustres** 1939

Aquatint, scraper and burin on copper, states III and IV

104

Cat. 81 **Woman in an Armchair/ Femme au fauteuil à balustres** 1939

Aquatint, scraper and burin on copper, states V and VI

Picasso's mother with other members of the family in Barcelona, ca. 1935 (Archives Vilato-Ruiz)

*Man with a Sheep*, 1943

Cat. 82 "Paris July 14th 1942"/ "Paris, 14 juillet 42"  14 July 1942  Etching (direct biting), scraper and burin on zinc, state V

# Exhibition checklist

(All works in the exhibition are on paper.)

1. **Torero Seen from the Back/ Torero de dos** Barcelona, ca. 1900 Woodcut 153 mm approximate diameter M.P. 3174 G/B 211 bis

2. **The Frugal Repast/ Le Repas frugal** Paris, September 1904 Etching and scraper on zinc 463 x 377 mm M.P. 1888 and 1889 G/B 2: I and II before steel facing

3 **The Saltimbanques/ Les Saltimbanques** Paris, spring-summer 1905 Drypoint on copper 288 x 326 mm M.P. 1896 G/B 9: II before steel facing

4. **Salome/ Salomé** Paris, late 1905 Drypoint on copper 400 x 348 mm M.P. 1903 G/B 17: III before steel facing

5.**Fernande Olivier/ Portrait de Fernande Olivier** Probably summer 1906 Drypoint on copper 162 x 118 mm M.P. 1905 G/B 18 bis

6. **Standing Nude/ Nu debout, mains croisées derrière le dos** Gosol or Paris, summer or autumn 1906 Monotype on glass 210 x 175 mm M.P. 3173 G/B 250

7. **Half-length Woman with Raised Hand/ Buste de femme à la main levée** Paris, autumn 1906 Woodcut 219 x 138 mm M.P. 3158 G/B 211

8. **Half-length Young Woman, three-quarters view/ Buste de jeune femme de trois quarts** Paris, autumn 1906 Woodcut 557 x 385 mm Proof pulled by the artist in 1933 M.P. 3159 G/B 212

9. **The Eagle/ L'Aigle** (for Apollinaire's *Bestiaire*) Paris, May–July 1907 Woodcut 83 x 78 mm M.P. 3160 G/B 213

10. **The Chick/ Le Poussin** (for Apollinaire's *Bestiaire*) Paris, May–July 1907 Woodcut 100 x 80 mm M.P. 3161 G/B 214

11. **Study for Nude with Drapery/ Etude pour** *Nu à la draperie* Paris, May–July 1907 Woodcut 219 x 138 mm M.P. 3167 G/B 218

12. **Study for Standing Nude/ Etude pour** *Nu debout* Paris, winter 1907–08 Woodcut 201 x 99 mm M.P. 3164 G/B 217

13. **Still Life with a Fruit Bowl/ Nature morte au compotier** Paris, winter 1908–09 Drypoint and scraper on copper 130 x 110 mm M.P. 1913 to 1915 G/B 22: I, II and after steel facing III

14. **Still Life with a Bottle of Marc/ Nature morte à la bouteille de marc** Paris, autumn 1911 Drypoint on copper 500 x 306 mm M.P. 1928 G/B 33 after steel facing

15. **Seated Guitar Player/ Guitariste au fauteuil** Paris, late 1911 and spring 1912 Etching and drypoint on copper 200 x 139 mm M.P. 1926 G/B 31: IV/V

16. **Guitar on a Table/ La Guitare sur la table** Paris, winter 1913–14 Woodcut 113 x 101 mm M.P. 3168 and 3169 G/B 220: I and II

17. **Man with a Pipe/ L'Homme à la pipe** Paris, end of 1914 or early 1915 Scraper, etching and drypoint on aquatinted zinc 75 x 54 mm M.P. 1973–78, 1980 and 1981 G/B 45: II–IX

18. **Two Women and a Nude Model/ Deux femmes regardant un modèle nu** Paris, autumn (?) 1923 Drypoint, scraper and etching on zinc 178 x 130 mm M.P. 2070 G/B 102: III/V, touched up in the press

19. **The Race/ La Course** 1924–25 Etching on zinc 118 x 78 mm M.P. 2053 G/B 92

20. **Seated Nude/ Femme assise, de face** 1924–25 Etching on zinc 118 x 78 mm M.P. 2054 G/B 93

21. **Standing Nude/ Femme accoudée en demi-figure** 1924–25 Etching on zinc 118 x 78 mm M.P. 2055 G/B 94

22. **Two Nudes Joining Hands/ Deux femmes nues se donnant la main** 1925 Etching on zinc 118 x 78 mm M.P. 2059 G/B 97: I/II

23. **Standing Nude/ Nu debout. III** 1925 Etching on zinc 118 x 78 mm M.P. 2051 G/B 90

24. **Standing Nude/ Nu debout. IV** 1925 Etching on zinc 118 x 78 mm M.P. 2052 G/B 91

25. **Standing Nude/ Femme nue debout** 1925 Monotype on zinc 118 x 60 mm M.P. 3178 G/B 256

26. **Dancer/ Danseuse** 1925 Monotype on zinc 118 x 60 mm M.P. 3179 G/B 257

27. **Bust of a Woman/ Buste de femme** Juan-les-Pins, summer, or probably Paris, autumn 1925 Etching on zinc 118 x 78 mm M.P. 2046 G/B 85

28. **Head of a Woman/ Tête de femme face et profil** Juan-les-Pins, summer, or probably Paris, autumn 1925 Etching on zinc 118 x 78 mm M.P. 2047 G/B 86

29. **Head of a Woman with Short Hair/ Tête de femme aux cheveux courts** Juan-les-Pins, summer, or probably Paris, autumn 1925 Etching on zinc 118 x 78 mm M.P. 2048 G/B 87

30. **Nude/ Femme nue aux traits parallèles** 1925 Etching on zinc 118 x 78 mm M.P. 2057 G/B 96

31. **Standing Nude, half-length/ Femme nue debout en demi-figure** Paris, late 1925 Etching on zinc 118 x 78 mm M.P. 2061 G/B 98

32. **Head of a Woman/ Tête de femme** Juan-les-Pins or Paris, second half of 1925 Etching on zinc 118 x 78 mm M.P. 2045 G/B 84

33. **Head of a Woman/ Tête sur un champ clair** Paris, winter 1925–26 Etching on zinc 118 x 78 mm M.P. 2064 G/B 100

34. The Death of the Bull/ La Mort du taureau Paris, 28 May 1929 Etching on copper 193 x 279 mm M.P. 2112 G/B 138

35. Study for *The Death of Orpheus* (Ovid's *Metamorphoses*)/ Etude pour *Mort d'Orphée* Juan-les-Pins, 1 September 1930 Pen and ink on paper 270 x 210 mm M.P. 1033 (recto)

36. The Death of Orpheus, I (Ovid's *Metamorphoses*)/ Mort d'Orphée. I Juan-les-Pins, 3 September 1930 Drypoint on copper Approximately 300 x 171 mm M.P. 2148 G/B 173

37. The Death of Orpheus, II/ Mort d'Orphée. II Boisgeloup, 16 September 1930 Etching on copper (pulled without the remarque) 312 x 221 mm M.P. 2150 G/B 174

38. The Death of Orpheus, III/ Mort d'Orphée. III Boisgeloup, 18 September 1930 Etching on copper 312 x 224 mm M.P. 2139 G/B 164

39. Marie-Thérèse in Profile/ Grand profil de Marie-Thérèse Probably 1931 Monotype on copper covered with a tarlatan 320 x 253 (size of the image) M.P. 3228 G/B 539

40. The Diver/ La Plongeuse Paris, 29 November 1932 Etching on copper 140 x 112 mm M.P. 2251 and 2253 G/B 277, printed with collage in 1936

(Four drypoints and etchings printed, recto and verso, on one sheet)
41A. The Rape/ Le Viol Paris, 21 November 1932 Drypoint on copper 123 x 91 mm M.P. 2199 G/B 264

41B. Bathers by the Sea/ Baigneuses sur la plage. II Paris, 22 November 1932 Etching on copper 121 x 92 mm M.P. 2199 G/B 266

41C. Bathers Playing by the Sea /Jeux au bord de la mer. Baigneuses. Paris, 29 November 1932 Etching on copper 140 x 113 mm M.P. 2199 G/B 262

41D. Marie-Thérèse Seated /Marie-Thérèse assise par terre Paris, 19 January 1933 Etching and drypoint on copper 149 x 96 mm M.P. 2199 G/B 285

(Four drypoints and etchings printed, recto and verso, on one sheet)
42A. Three Bathers. The Three Graces / Trois baigneuses. Les trois Grâces Paris, 7 December 1932 Etching on copper 141 x 113 mm M.P. 2271 G/B 280

42B. Bather Opening a Beach Cabana Door. The Rain/ Baigneuse à la cabine. L'averse Paris, 19 January 1933 Drypoint on copper 144 x 75 mm M.P. 2271 G/B 286, II

42C. Monument. Head of Marie-Thérèse on a Column/ Monument. Tête de Marie-Thérèse sur une colonne Paris, 5 March 1933 Etching, scraper, burnisher and drypoint on copper 125 x 29 mm M.P. 2271 G/B 291, XIII

42D. Sleeping Woman and Flute Player/ Dormeuse et flûtiste Paris, 6 March 1933 Drypoint and etching on copper 88 x 80 mm M.P. 2271 G/B 292, III

43. Marie-Thérèse in Profile, II/ Marie-Thérèse de profil. II Paris, 2 January 1933 Monotype on copper 235 x 205 mm (size of the image) M.P. 3186 G/B 449

44. The Storm/ L'Orage Paris, 18 January 1933 Etching on copper 179 x 145 mm M.P. 2279 G/B 284

45. Flute Player and Sleeping Woman /Flûtiste et dormeuse Paris, 24 January–early February 1933 Drypoint on copper 150 x 187 mm M.P. 2288–2290, 2295–2314, 2316–2319, 2321–2324, 2331 G/B 287: I–XVIII, XX–XXV, XXVII–XXX, XXXI

46. Flute Player and Sleeping Woman/ Flûtiste et dormeuse Paris, February 1933 Monotype on copper 150 x 187 mm M.P. 3193, 3195, 3197, 3200, 3201, 3203, 3205, 3207, 3209, 3211, 3213, 3216, 3218, 3220, 3221, 3223 G/B 494–509

47. Sculptural Profile of Marie-Thérèse/ Profil sculptural de Marie-Thérèse Paris, 16 February 1933 Monotype on copper 318 x 228 mm M.P. 3230 G/B 554 (see 50; same plate)

48. Sculpture. Head of Marie-Thérèse/ Sculpture. Tête de Marie-Thérèse Paris, 18 February 1933 Drypoint and scraper on copper 320 x 229 mm M.P. 2335–2338, 2339–2345, 2347–2350, 2354, 2357, 2358, 2360 G/B 288: I–XX

49. Sculpture. Head of Marie-Thérèse/ Sculpture. Tête de Marie-Thérèse Paris, February 1933 Monotype on copper 318 x 227 mm M.P. 3231, 3233, 3234, 3236 G/B 555–557 (printed from G/B 288: IV) and 558 (printed from G/B 288: XX)

50. Sculptural Profile of Marie-Thérèse/Profil sculptural de Marie-Thérèse Paris, 7 March 1933 Etching and drypoint on copper 318 x 228 mm M.P. 2381, 2384, 2383 G/B 294: II and III (touched up in the press) and III (reworked with lithographic crayon)

51. Sculpture. Profile of Marie-Thérèse / Sculpture. Profil de Marie-Thérèse Paris, 12 March 1933 Before biting; inking and monotype made over ground stopped out with Marie-Thérèse's nail polish 176 x 155 mm M.P. 2385 G/B 295

52. Sculptor and Model with a Mirror/ Sculpteur et modèle se regardant dans un miroir calé sur un autoportrait sculpté Paris, 8 April 1933 Etching on copper 368 x 299 mm M.P. 2623 G/B 331 before steel facing (proof pulled by Lacourière around 1934–35)

53. Standing Minotaur with a Dagger/ Minotaur au poignard debout Paris, 11 April 1933 Etching on copper 268 x 194 mm M.P. 2392 G/B 337, heightened with gouache and collage

54. The Embrace/ L'Etreinte. II Boisgeloup, 23 April 1933 Drypoint on copper 300 x 366 mm M.P. 2393 G/B/ 339 before steel facing (proof pulled by Lacourière in 1934 or 1935)

55. Marie-Thérèse Dreaming of Metamorphoses/ Marie-Thérèse rêvant de métamorphoses: elle-même et le sculpteur buvant avec un jeune acteur grec jouant le rôle du minotaure Boisgeloup, 18 June 1933 (I) and end of 1934 Drypoint, etching, scraper and burin on copper 298 x 365 mm M.P. 2403, 2670–2672 G/B 368: I–IV before steel facing (proofs pulled by Lacourière in 1934 and 1935)

56. **Minotaur and Sleeping Woman/ Minotaure caressant du mufle la main d'une dormeuse** Boisgeloup, 18 June 1933 (III) and end of 1934 for second state Drypoint on copper 299 x 365 mm M.P. 2674 G/B 369: II before steel facing

57. **Copulation, II/ Accouplement. II** Paris, 3 November 1933 Etching and drypoint on copper 199 x 278 mm M.P. 2411 and 2414 G/B 379: I and IV before steel facing

58. **Rembrandt with Marie-Thérèse as His Model/ Rembrandt à la palette avec Marie-Thérèse comme modèle** Paris, 18 February 1934 Etching, drypoint and scraper on copper 138.5 x 207 mm M.P. 2436 and 2442 G/B 420: I and VII before steel facing (proof pulled by Lacourière around 1934–35)

59. **Women Together with a Sculpture-Voyeur (after Ingres)/ Femmes entres elles, avec voyeur sculpté (d'après le *Bain Turc*)** Paris, 10 March 1934 and late 1934 Etching, scraper and burin on copper 223 x 316 mm M.P. 2645–2647, 2649 G/B 424: I and III–V before steel facing (proofs pulled by Lacourière at the end of 1934)

60. **Female Matador. Last Kiss?/ Femme torero. Dernier baiser?** Paris, 12 June 1934 Etching on copper 497 x 697 mm M.P. 2446 G/B 425

61. **The Death of Marat/ Le Mort de Marat** Paris or Boisgeloup, 21 July 1934 Drypoint and burin on copper Approximately 135 x 107 mm (size of the image) M.P. 2451–2454 G/B 430: III, four proofs in colour

62. **The Great Corrida with Female Matador/ La Grande Corrida, avec femme torero** Boisgeloup, 8 September 1934 Etching on copper 497 x 697 mm M.P. 2460 G/B 433

63. **Catalan Fishermen on a Spree in a Tavern/ En la taberna. Pêcheurs catalans en bordée** Paris, 11 November 1934 Etching on copper 235 x 297 mm M.P. 2464 G/B 439, printed with collage, perhaps in 1936

64. **Two Masked Figures before a Harpy Perched on a Low Column/ Chez la Pythie-Harpye. Homme au masque de minotaure et femme au masque de sculpteur** Paris, 19 November 1934 Aquatint on copper 248 x 348 mm M.P. 2512 G/B 441, proof before steel facing

65. **Marie-Thérèse as an Idol and Three Bearded Greeks/ Marie-Thérèse en idole et trois Grecs barbus** Paris, 19 November–7 December 1934 Sugar lift aquatint, scraper, burin and etching on copper 129 x 179 mm M.P. 2513 and 2520 G/B 416: I and VI before steel facing

66. **Sheet of Studies: Seated Nude and Head of a Bearded Man/ Feuille d'études: Barbu et femme assise de dos** Paris, 27 December 1934 Etching on screened celluloid 189 x 146 mm M.P. 2466 G/B 443

67. **Blind Minotaur in the Night/ Minotaure aveugle guidé par Marie-Thérèse au pigeon dans une nuit étoilée** Paris, 3–7 to 31 December 1934 and/or 1 January 1935 Aquatint, scraper, drypoint and burin on copper 247 x 348 mm M.P. 2702 G/B 437: IV, before steel facing, printed in colour

68. **The Minotauromachy/ La Minotauromachie** Paris, 23 March–3 May 1935 Etching, scraper and burin on copper 494/498 x 687/693 mm M.P. 2726–2728, 2730–2733 BAER 573 and *Addendum*: I–IV, VI, VII, and VII (both VII after steel facing, one printed in colour)

69. **Faun Unveiling a Sleeping Woman/ Faune dévoilant une dormeuse** Paris, 12 June 1936 Aquatint, scraper and burin on copper 316 x 417 mm M.P. 2526–2531 BAER 609: I–VI before steel facing

70. **Ambroise Vollard/ Portrait of Vollard. IV** Paris, 4 March 1937 Etching, aquatint and scraper on copper 345 x 246 mm M.P. 2740 BAER 620: I/II

71. **Weeping Woman, I/ La Femme qui pleure. I** Paris, 1 July 1937 Drypoint, aquatint, etching and scraper on copper 692 x 495 mm M.P. 2741–2743, 2745, 2746, 2749, 2747 BAER 623: I/VII and *Addendum*

72. **Weeping Woman, III/ La Femme qui pleure. III** Paris, 4 July 1937 (I) Drypoint and aquatint on copper 348 x 247 mm M.P. 2775 BAER 625

73. **Weeping Woman, IV/ La Femme qui pleure. IV** Paris, 4 July 1937 (II) Drypoint on copper 347 x 250 mm M.P. 2776 BAER 626

74. **Dora Maar, I/ Portrait de Dora Maar. I** Mougins, 15 August 1937 Monotype on copper

349 x 254 mm M.P. 2757 BAER 712, pulled from unworked copper of BAER 627

75. **Dora Maar, II/ Portrait de Dora Maar. II** Mougins, 15 August 1937 Monotype on copper, with collage of flowers 349 x 254 mm M.P. 2758 BAER 713: see also BAER 627

76. **Dora Maar Wearing a Necklace/ Dora Maar au collier** Paris, 7 October 1937 Drypoint on copper 415 x 317 mm M.P. 2760 BAER 628 (retouched in the press, in colour)

77. **Bust of a Seated Woman/ Buste de femme à la chaise** (Plate for Breton's *Anthologie de l'humour noir*) Paris, 18 October 1938 Etching, aquatint, scraper and burin on copper 248 x 138 mm (with the text) 195 x 138 mm (without text) M.P. 2780, 2782, 2784, 2785 BAER 643: I, III, IX, IX, (the latter with collage), and X (private collection)

78. **The Woman with a Tambourine/ La Femme au tambourin** Paris, between 15 and 31 January 1939 Aquatint and scraper on copper 658 x 510 mm M.P. 2788, 2789 and 2792–2794 BAER 646: I–V

79. **Woman Wearing a Hat Seated in an Armchair/ Femme au fauteuil et au chapeau** Paris, March 1939 Aquatint, scraper and burin, in five colours, on five separate copperplates 299 x 238 mm M.P. 2879, 2886, 2888, 2891, 2897, 2896, 2894, 2895, 2900, 2901, 2903, 2904, 2902, 2898, 2905, 2907, 2911, 2906, 2912, 2908, 2914, 2913, 2909, 2919, 2899, 2916, 2917, 2918 BAER 647: progressive separations for the five colours (red, black, green, blue and yellow) and various states of superposition of colours

80.(*Small prints for a book conceived by Vollard and Sabartés*)
1. **Standing Nude, I** and **Small Standing Nude/ Nu debout. I** and **Petit Nu debout** Paris, 25–27 April 1939 Burin and aquatint; burin; on two copperplates 295 x 96 mm; 296 x 51 mm M.P. 2872 BAER 656: IV and 657

2. **Standing Nude, II/ Nu debout. II** Paris, 1 May 1939 Burin and aquatint on two copperplates, one used for colour 247 x 74.5 (black) and 299x 125 mm (colour) M.P. 2865 BAER 658: II

3. **Walking Nude/ Femme nue marchant les mains sur la tête** Paris, ca. 1 May 1939 Burin and aquatint on copper 309 x 67 mm M.P. 2864 BAER 659 **Standing Nude, II/ Nu debout. II** Paris, 1 May 1939 Burin on copper 247 x 74.5 mm M.P. 2864 BAER 658: I

4. **Head of a Woman/ Tête de femme de trois quarts** Paris, 2 May 1939 Burin and drypoint on two copperplates, one used for colour 297 x 112 mm (colour) and 202 x 66 mm (black) M.P. 2875 BAER 660

5. **(Poem, no. 34)/ "XXXIV. El clarin se retuerce..."** Paris, 9 May 1939 Etching, scraper and burin on copper around a héliogravure reproduction of the artist's manuscript writing 447 x 338 mm (size of the image) M.P. 3036 BAER 661: III

6. **Bather with a Towel, I/ Baigneuse à la serviette. I** Paris, 15 May 1939 Burin and aquatint on copper 245 x 67 mm M.P. 2868 BAER 662: III

7. **Bather with a Towel, III/ Baigneuse à la serviette. III** Paris, 17 May 1939 Burin and aquatint, in four colours, on four copperplates 238 x 101 mm M.P. 2867 BAER 664

8. **Bather with a Ball and Towel/ Baigneuse à la balle et à la serviette** Paris, May (?) 1939 Aquatint, scraper and burin on copper 238 x 102 mm M.P. 2870 BAER 665: II/III

9. **(Female Figures and Printed Words)/ Trozo de almibar** Paris, 9 June 1939 Burin on copper 348 x 245.5 mm M.P. 3034 BAER 667

81. **Woman in an Armchair/ Femme au fauteuil à balustres** Paris, January–June 1939 Aquatint, scraper and burin on copper 342 x 222 mm M.P. 2808–2813 BAER 670: I–VI before steel facing

82. **"Paris July 14th 1942"/ "Paris, 14 juillet 42"** Paris, 14 July 1942 Etching (direct biting), scraper and burin on zinc 452 x 641 mm M.P. 2953 BAER 682: V

## Woodblocks

6. **Study for *Standing Nude*** (M.P. 3544)

16. **Guitar on a Table** (M.P. 3545)

## Copper Plates

68. **Minotauromachy** (M.P. 3527)

71. **Weeping Woman, I** (M.P. 3528)

78. **The Woman with a Tambourine** (M.P. 1982–54)

79. **Woman Wearing a Hat Seated in an Armchair** (five copper plates) (M.P. 3536–3540)